# SILVER SCREEN
# SILVER PRINTS

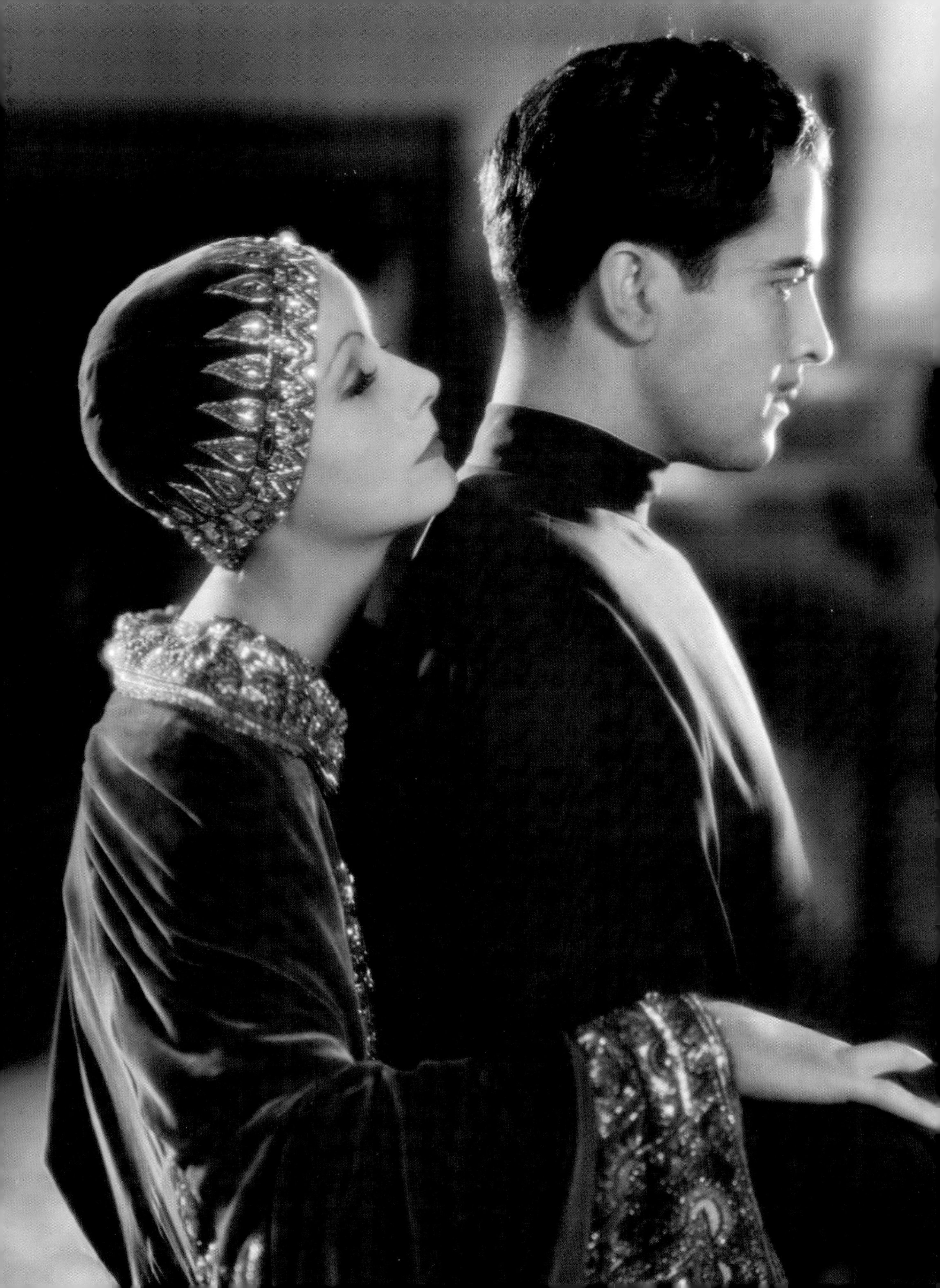

# SILVER SCREEN SILVER PRINTS

## Hollywood Glamour Portraits from the Robert Dance Collection

ANNE H. HOY

The Grolier Club
New York
2011

An exhibition at The Grolier Club
September 13–November 12, 2011



ISBN: 978-1-60583-035-3

COVER
Ruth Harriet Louise, *Greta Garbo,* 1927, for *The Divine Woman,* gelatin silver print

FRONTISPIECE
Milton Brown, *Greta Garbo and Ramon Novarro,* 1931, for *Mata Hari,* gelatin silver print

# Contents

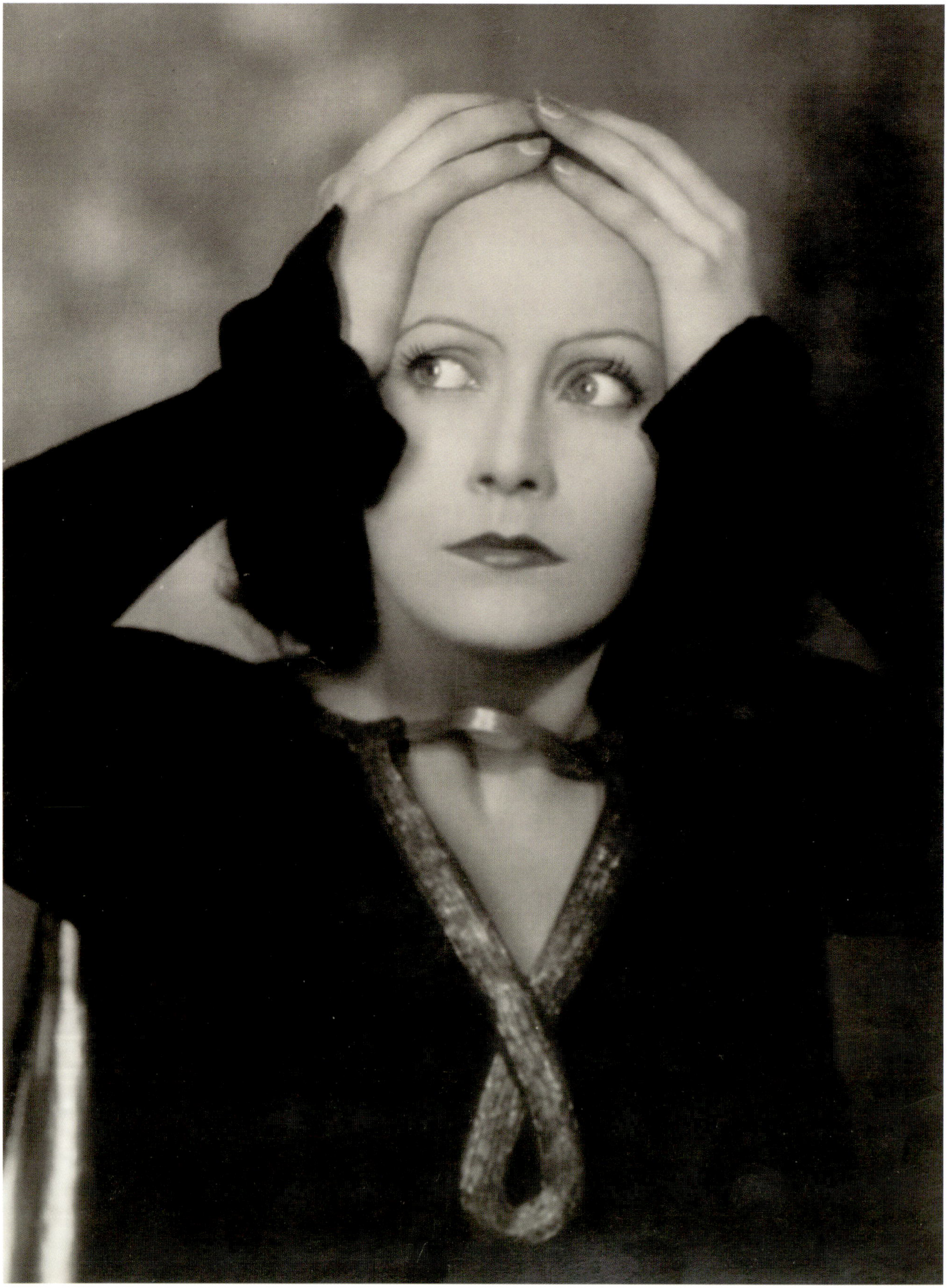

# Introduction & Acknowledgments

*Silver Screen/Silver Prints: Hollywood Glamour Portraits from the Robert Dance Collection* sketches a genre of portraiture special to Hollywood in its Golden Age. Luminous black-and-white close-ups of the goddesses and gods of filmdom between the wars, these photographs were central to creating the stars' public personas and they guided the cinematographers who elaborated them on screen. Because portrait photographers were part of each studio's publicity machine and thus subordinate to its performers and films, the names of the leading portrait artists—Ruth Harriet Louise, Clarence Bull, George Hurrell, and Eugene Richee, for example—remain little known, certainly by comparison to those of art and fashion photographers in the same decades. This catalogue and the exhibition it accompanies are intended to direct a fresh spotlight on Hollywood's portraitists, whose ravishing vintage prints were reproduced in the gamut of print forms for media and for legions of fans, satisfying as they heightened a mass longing for glamour and escape at a time of drastic economic and social change.

Since the Grolier Club founders dedicated themselves to promoting all the arts relating to books, including prints and other works on paper, and began sharing their own collections with the public, the Club has hosted a number of stimulating and visually engaging exhibitions that explore cultural phenomena as seen in print. *The Enchantress: Emma, Lady Hamilton* (from the Jean Kislak collection) and *Quack! Quack! Quack! Sellers of Nostrums in Prints, Posters, Ephemera, and Books* (from the William Helfand collection) are but two recent examples surveying popular fascinations that generated engrossing works on paper and memorable images. *Silver Screen/Silver Prints* has some of those qualities, though its contents are closer to us in time. Is the beauty who entranced a national hero not unlike the beauties who entranced a nation? At the same time, one might smile from a distance at the youthful happiness and health promised by medical advertising. The elixirs of Belle Époque pharmacology and the faces of Golden Age Hollywood are charming fictions, both the Helfand and Dance collections say, distancing fears of disease and the Depression. The Helfand holdings show gems of the popular medium of the day, the color lithograph; the Dance collection highlights in vintage gelatin silver photographs the twentieth-century medium par excellence. Each exhibition with its catalogue serves to highlight how popular images can express a mass yearning and give it memorable form.

That the Grolier Club's wealth lies in its members is again demonstrated in such exhibitions. These displays underscore the fact that individual collectors are often the engines of scholarship, ahead of institutions. These grand acquisitors are near-obsessed pursuers of sometimes unlikely quarry, and in sharing their obsessions with the public they assure that their continued quest will become even more difficult, especially as others learn from their discerning tastes. We are indebted to Robert Dance as the latest in a distinguished line. The Club's history of fine

Ruth Harriet Louise, *Greta Garbo,* 1927

exhibitions is laden with his predecessors, and its public programming would be pale and thin without them.

Finally, *Silver Screen/Silver Prints* could not have taken place without the Club's bedrock of volunteers. Our colleagues assured that this exhibition, like those they have mounted over the years, was presented as expertly as the displays of fine art at the largest New York institutions. They furthered the goals of the Club's public exhibitions committee, whose imagination and experience are warmly acknowledged here. Working with Club director Eric Holzenberg, exhibitions coordinator Megan Smith, and administrative assistant Maev Brennan, these Club members expertly supported this guest curator at every turn.

All these volunteers assisted the most dedicated volunteer of all, the collector himself—who was involved in every aspect of *Silver Screen/Silver Prints* and provided the research for the catalogue sections of the publication. At Dartmouth in the 1970s, Robert Dance took film studies courses taught by the son of Harry Rapf, a founder of MGM, and heard luminaries such as director King Vidor and critic Pauline Kael begin to create the first academic history of Hollywood. Around 1980 he bought his first photograph, from pioneering photography dealer Lee Witkin. It was a portrait of Garbo by Ruth Harriet Louise. Neither man knew who Louise was. As Dance pursued a career as an art dealer specializing in sixteenth- and seventeenth-century artists, he applied the same art connoisseurship to studying Hollywood photography and he continued collecting photographs alongside British mezzotints and modern illustrated books. Frustrated that he could find little information about Louise, he researched her biography himself: his monograph on Louise was published in 2002. This was followed by two more volumes on the glamour genre in photography, each accompanied by an international traveling exhibition.

Old Master painters and studio photographers both work from "a well-established iconography," Dance says. "The celebrities of the Renaissance and the Baroque are saints and mythological heros: Saints Barbara and Sebastian are always beautiful; in mythology Apollo contrasts with Hercules. As the world became more secularized in the industrial era, society became a fascination for the middle class; think of popular mezzotint portraits of Lady Hamilton, a figure as unattainable to the common viewer as the saints in earlier times. In the twentieth century it was the movies and the stars."

Dance's latest acquisition is an 8 x 10-inch negative by Louise of Garbo, shown full-length in evening dress. This unique work is as close to a relic of the two women as photography permits. Louise's studio lights and sheet film captured the image of the actress at a particular moment in early 1926. Garbo was twenty. The negative shows no retouching. In this recent prize of Dance's thirty-year absorption, we recognize an interwar cultural construct that is simultaneously a magical artwork and an irreplaceable artifact of a star.

—AHH

New York, August 2011

# SILVER SCREEN
# SILVER PRINTS

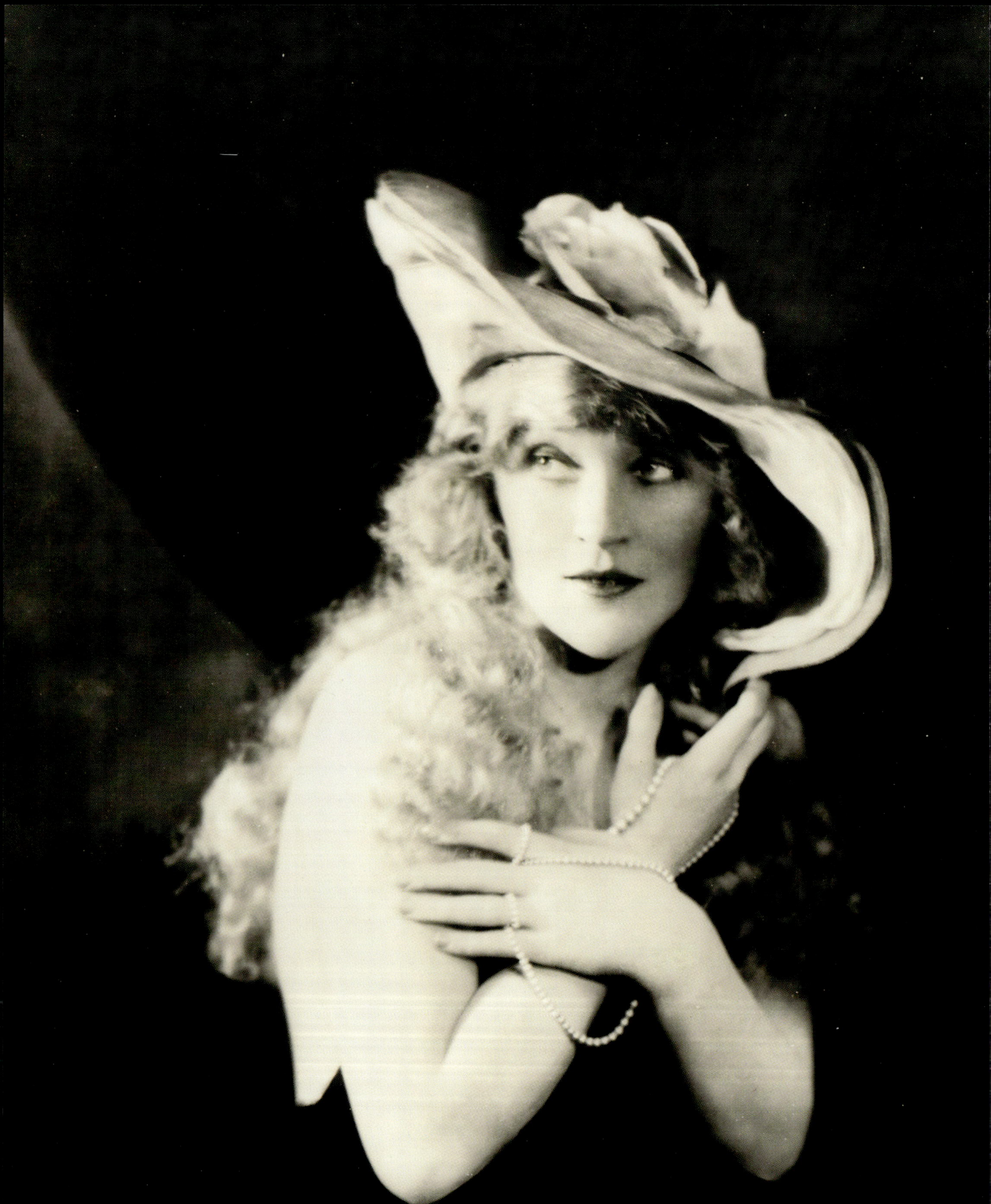

# "I'm Ready for My Close-up": Hollywood's Glamour Photographs

ANNE H. HOY

*"What people remember of those stars is not from films, but* one *essential photo: Dietrich heavy-lidded, sucked-in cheeks/Keaton—sad little boy/Crawford—staring self-admiration/ Gable—smiling, darling. And when I think of Garbo I do not see her moving in any particular film. I see her staring mysteriously into the camera. No matter how many times I've seen her in films, that is how I always see her. She is a still picture—unchangeable."*

—actress Louise Brooks[1]

For several good reasons Louise Brooks remembered Garbo as a single, iconic photograph, not as an actress performing in a favorite motion picture. Memories of graphically simple black-and-white images may be more easily imprinted than sequences of movement. Certainly movie stills and their loftier cousins, glamour portraits, were more common than film clips in Hollywood's pre-YouTube era. Sheer repetition strengthened the aesthetic potency of these photographs, radiant images that appeared in virtually every print medium. Apart from the films of the 1920s and '30s that they promoted, these silver prints were Hollywood's most powerful fabrications, telling a generation of viewers across social classes how to kiss, how to dress, how to succeed, what to dream.

The glamour photograph was not Hollywood's invention pure and simple. But Hollywood perfected it and promulgated it most widely. It was unmistakably distinct from a portrait of the real Lucille LeSueur (Joan Crawford). It was not necessarily a portrayal of Garbo in her latest role (though the reclusive Swede retreated behind her period costumes when she disliked a studio photographer). And it was certainly not a candid of Gloria Swanson caught unaware of the camera. In fact, the glamour photograph, and the Golden Age of Hollywood that it epitomized, both faded with the expansion of tabloid tastes and the swarming of paparazzi around 1960.

Rather, the glamour photograph summed up stardom as brilliant, magical, remote, yet visually accessible, and furthered this entrancing fiction for mostly female fans between the

*Mae Murray*, cat. no. 2

world wars. Distinct from today's fleeting celebrity shot, created in dedicated photography studios apart from the movie sets, it captured the intersection of individual and type—of Clara Bow as the It Girl, of Lillian Gish as the adorable waif, of Jean Harlow as the blonde bombshell, of Joan Crawford as the New Woman, and Marlene Dietrich as the world-weary *femme fatale* (pages 13, 21, 48). Starting with beauties enhanced by dental work (sometimes) and cosmetics (almost always), this photograph was made with the best cameras, lights, and retouchers that money could buy. Perhaps even more than filmmaking, it represented the control exerted on performers by Hollywood's "Studio System" in force from the mid-1920s through the early 1960s—notably those contracts covering the stars' performances, monopolizing all publicity, and thereby shaping and rationing all available images on-screen and off.

The selections from the Robert Dance collection in this catalogue and the exhibition it accompanies let us appraise a seductive chapter in American portrait photography, celebrity culture, and popular art.

## The Studios' Portrait Studios

In 1936 a *New York Times* article described "The cinema's glamour machine that takes waitresses, debutantes, actresses, schoolgirls and their masculine parallels and by adroit veneering makes of them the dream children of the silver screen." It credited filmdom's powers of transformation to "the still department."[2] *The Times* meant the portrait studio, a branch of the publicity department at each of the major motion picture companies.[3]

There a screen hopeful was sent, even before a screen test, to be photographed in makeup and assorted costumes, to be found photogenic—or not—on the ground glass of an 8 x 10-inch view camera. The sheet film was less expensive than motion picture stock; the lighting and staging could be controlled by the photographer, perhaps with one assistant, rather than necessitating a crew. And the resulting portraits would determine whether a screen test was worthwhile and if so how the cinematographer might proceed, while they were also added to casting books, compilations intended to help executives match scripted characters to flesh-and-blood performers. "The player photographing most nearly like the director's mental picture," wrote G. R. Mook in *Silver Screen* (September 1935), "gets the part."

Once an actress or actor signed a contract, the studio began to craft an image with a biography and a portrait sitting, and an eye to the recent successes at competing studios. (Clark Gable was groomed to compete with Gary Cooper; Anna Sten was supposed to match Dietrich.) For established stars and the lesser "featured players," new portraits were a vital contact with print media and their fans—to build excitement about a film in production or on view, and to keep their images alive in the public imagination between films. As soon as costumes were ready or the filming was complete, portrait sessions could be scheduled, for a few hours or as much as a full day or two.

*Joan Crawford,* cat. no. 59

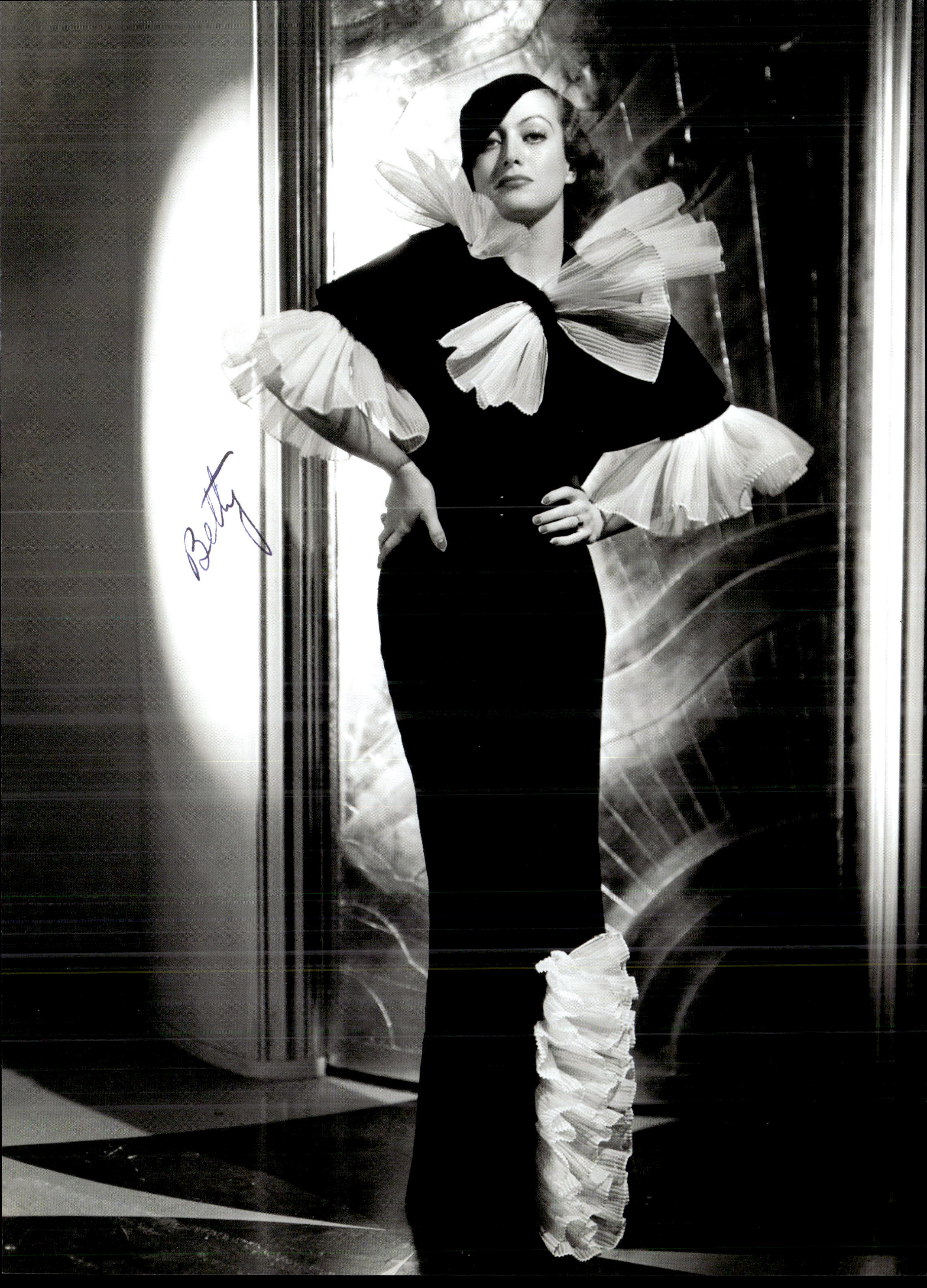
Betty

After exhaustive retouching, cropping, and enlarging, studio portraitists often made 11 x 14-inch prints of their favorite images, sometimes with sepia toning, and stamped or signed them for studio executives, the stars, the fan magazines, and themselves. After the round of approvals, hundreds of thousands of prints were made from the original 8 x 10-inch negatives or copy negatives and mailed out—by the stars themselves, the studios' publicity departments, or monthlies like *Photoplay.* "The cost of publicizing players is astounding," the 1935 *Silver Screen* story went on. "Salaries in the PR department of a major studio run between $150,000 and $250,000 a year. The New York office is half that. The 'Still Gallery' where the portraits are made costs around $100,000 a year to maintain." By contrast in these Depression years, Hollywood also sang, "Brother, Can You Spare a Dime?"

During filming, on the sound stages or on location, stills were taken with portable cameras during breaks in the action. Recapturing scenes that had just been shot, these photographs could be used for publicity and to document the filmmaking to assure continuity. Frame blowups—prints made from the film itself—served the same purpose. Yet neither stills nor frame blowups rivaled the focused artistry of the glamour portraits, or the voluptuous quality of the 11 x 14-inch vintage images, printed by the photographers themselves.

The cinematographer's first purpose was (and is) time-based story-telling with a director and a cast and crew of dozens, perhaps thousands, not the creation of icons one by one. The motion picture camera was bulky, and during the transition to sound pictures it was housed with recording equipment and thus even bulkier, making close-ups impossible. Motion picture film was not retouched. Furthermore, on-set and on-location relationships lacked the flexibility and intimacy of the portrait studio (Figure 1). That intimacy deepened over a star's career. While a director and cinematographer would often change with each film,[4] the studio photographer was a long-running part of a performer's life.

Early directors recognized the power of the portrait photograph, and especially the close-up. Post-production portraits of Lillian Gish by Manhattan photographer Hendrick Sartov were reportedly so compelling for *Hearts of the World* (1918), for example, that

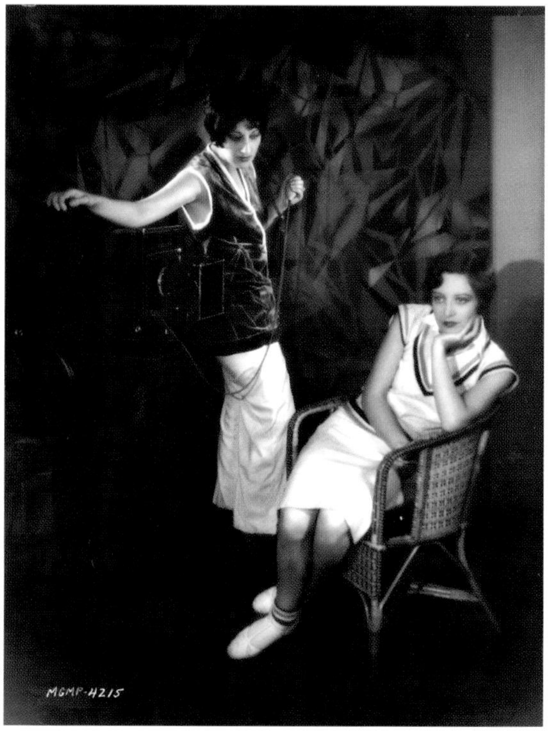


FIGURE 1
Clarence Sinclair Bull, *Ruth Harriet Louise photographing Joan Crawford,* 1928.
Courtesy John Kobal Foundation.

director D.W. Griffith had him make close-ups of her that were inserted into the already completed film. The billboard images prepared from glamour photographs of Gary Cooper and Helen Hayes for *A Farewell to Arms* (1932) influenced the director Frank Borzage in shooting the love scenes.[5]

What helped generate such riveting images were the time-honored portrait traditions that gallery photographers evoked, from Van Dyck to Sargent to fashion photography's Baron de Meyer, as well as art history's iconography of beauty, of Venus and the Virgin, Hercules and the dandy. The debts are most obvious in the late 'teens and early '20s when the film industry was young and Pictorialist photography (which openly imitated painting) offered the most alluring graphic sources. By the late '20s, however, modernist photography had come to dominate much vanguard art, and the Hollywood glamour photograph emerged as a specialty within it.

## Venus via Ziegfeld

"Glorifying the American Girl" was on the masthead of the Ziegfeld Follies, presented on Forty-second Street, New York, with new shows annually from 1913 to 1931. Broadway was Hollywood's creative mother lode in those years, and the talent found by the impresario Florenz Ziegfeld moonlighted in films or migrated to Hollywood—its beauties, chorus girls, singers, dancers, and comedians. Even earlier, both vaudeville and serious plays were supporting New York photography studios, which supplied publicity images for media and fans.

Alfred Cheney Johnston was one of the early links between Broadway and Hollywood, as he made arty but inviting images of Follies Girls and headlined stars in c. 1916–31. He and Ziegfeld were known as "the Siamese twins of beauty," Johnston combining art school training with early camera practice in the Sarony Studio (established in 1866, the first to specialize in theatrical photographs).[6] He poses former Follies Girl Mae Murray with the conventions of Susannah surprised in her bath but wearing pearls and a Gainsborough hat (page 10). The Susannah or modest Venus pose was then a coy commonplace that let artists bring pretty hands up to the bosom and accent hourglass silhouettes—especially in full-length versions with a bent knee. Johnston's side lighting, primarily from a window, brightens the new film star's long curls.

Johnston's counterparts in the 'teens, as seen in the Dance collection, included Arthur Rice, James Abbe, Russell Ball, and George Cannons. In the interchanges between painting, film, and photography that they fostered, Rice vignetted Alla Nazimova in the silent-picture equivalent of a cameo to accent her astonishing headdress in *Salomé* (1923, page 29). Following "screen royalty" Mary Pickford and Douglas Fairbanks on holiday in Paris, Abbe seated them in a garden with rhyming limbs and a garland behind their heads. Whether through exoticism, lavish dress, or decorous art references, these portraits obscured the humble sources of Broadway and Hollywood in girlie shows, itinerant thespians, and Edison's Kinetoscopes.

## Garbo, Louise, and Steichen

For Arnold Genthe, Garbo was a dramatic actress (page 36); for MGM's Ruth Harriet Louise she was a star (page 6, cover). In her dark half-length by Genthe, an independent photographer, taken a month after her arrival in New York in summer 1925, the bushy-haired Scandinavian strikes a twisted pose with a histrionic gesture and ominous glance. This photographer of Isadora Duncan and her troupe may have recalled their drastic movements, or perhaps he was impressed by Garbo's credentials from the Swedish Royal Academy of Dramatic Art. In any case, Genthe's interpretation suited the high-end cultural magazine *Vanity Fair* and a print was reproduced with word she was about to begin work on her first American picture, for Metro-Goldwyn.[7] The photograph had no aesthetic influence.

In Louise's Culver City studio in early fall, however, Garbo tilts her head back, her white fox collar caressing her cheek, while side lighting accents her now-soft hair and swan neck. Her vague sidelong glance and open lips signal erotic longing. She is already embodying "The Divine Woman," though Louise's luminous, simpler, soft-focus portraits of her lay ahead, in the fall 1927 production of that film.[8] As head of MGM's portrait studio from 1925 to late 1929, Louise would establish Garbo's screen persona, identifying her dramatic intensity with devouring romantic ardor, sometimes ecstatic, sometimes melancholy.

Louise's image of Garbo is not the star's most famous, however. When Edward Steichen was sent to Hollywood for *Vanity Fair* in 1928 and got his indelible image of Garbo staring into his lens, her black-clad arms and dress framing her face, he got lucky (Figure 2). Her gesture had been caught in a portrait by Louise, published a year before, and enacted in the film *Love* (1927) (page 6). As Robert Dance points out in his monograph on Louise, the gesture doubtless came from Garbo's dramatic academy exercises;[9] it was also exaggerated in early silent films, in which tragic heroines tear their hair or raise their fists to their tear-stained faces. Dance concludes: "Steichen's vision of Garbo, which he treats as romantically fresh [in his *A Life in Photography*, 1963, and earlier] is in reality a product of both Garbo's experience and the skill of her previous photographers."[10]

Such scholarship is needed to sort out the interchanges between Louise and her MGM colleagues and Steichen during his career as Condé Nast's best-paid photographer, generating monthly celebrity portraits and fashion photographs for *Vanity Fair* and *Vogue* from 1923 to 1938.[11] What may be most illuminating are the reasons for the success of Garbo's iconic image. In these and subsequent similar portrayals her gesture simultaneously sets off her nobly proportioned face while withholding her body: she remains legendary for her insistence on privacy in the most personally invasive of professions. In her film romances she embodied all-consuming passion but somehow without carnality. The simplest of the portraits, Steichen's monumentalizes Garbo's face on a pyramid of arms and draped chair back, printed darkly to form an irregular flat shape. High side-lighting directs attention to her brow and slightly troubled gaze at us.

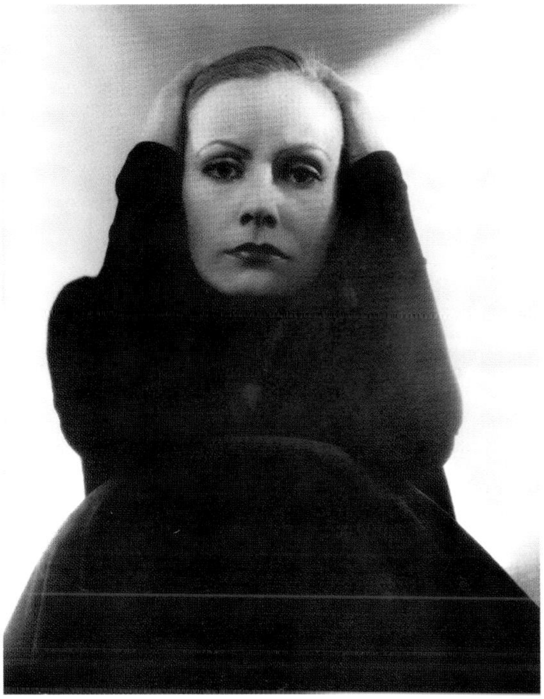

FIGURE 2
Edward Steichen, *Greta Garbo,* 1928.
Courtesy Santa Barbara Museum of Art.

Here are the mystery and reticence of the star, captured with minimalist modernism. Close-up and composition coincide with a potent characterization—which Steichen condensed from Louise's example.

In his exhibitions and books, Steichen lost no opportunity to include his Hollywood portraits, adding their glamour to his own, while his early fine art photography and association with Alfred Stieglitz enhanced his commercial standing in the '20s and '30s. By contrast, Louise and her MGM colleague Clarence Sinclair Bull and her successor George Hurrell had fewer opportunities for self-promotion, and their artistry was only widely recognized seventy-some years later.[12] Steichen's stark modernist idiom became his Condé Nast trademark, one in which society women, fashion models, literati, and performers participated, but Louise's style always served her film subjects' personalities as she, they, and her MGM superiors collaborated in marketing them for a mass audience. Louise and her cohort of contract photographers were valued for their productivity—she produced a hundred thousand negatives in her less than five years at MGM—and their versatility. On the other hand, Steichen and his peers, such as George Hoyningen-Huene, Cecil Beaton, and Man Ray, succeeded commercially by ringing small changes on signature styles.[13]

In Hollywood photography any signature belonged to the star, not the photographer. And the studios' demands for novelty to feed publicity machines discouraged the creation of distinctive camera styles. As seen in the Robert Dance collection, Louise's responses ranged from high-art allusions to kitsch and snapshot-style spontaneity. In one photograph an Expressionist "mask" of actress Eleanor Boardman looms from a black ground and displays stylized emotion (page 38). For the European market, perceived as more sophisticated than the American one, Louise reduced Garbo to a dark profile silhouette. At the opposite extreme, among amusing seasonal pictures, she costumed Crawford to flaunt her dancer's long legs as Santa's helper. "At home" staged candids included Marion Davies in her Santa Monica beach-house garden. In the '30s, now independent, Louise adapted the hard-edged style of Hurrell, who replaced her at MGM in January 1930: witness stylish Myrna Loy in satin gloves (page 40).

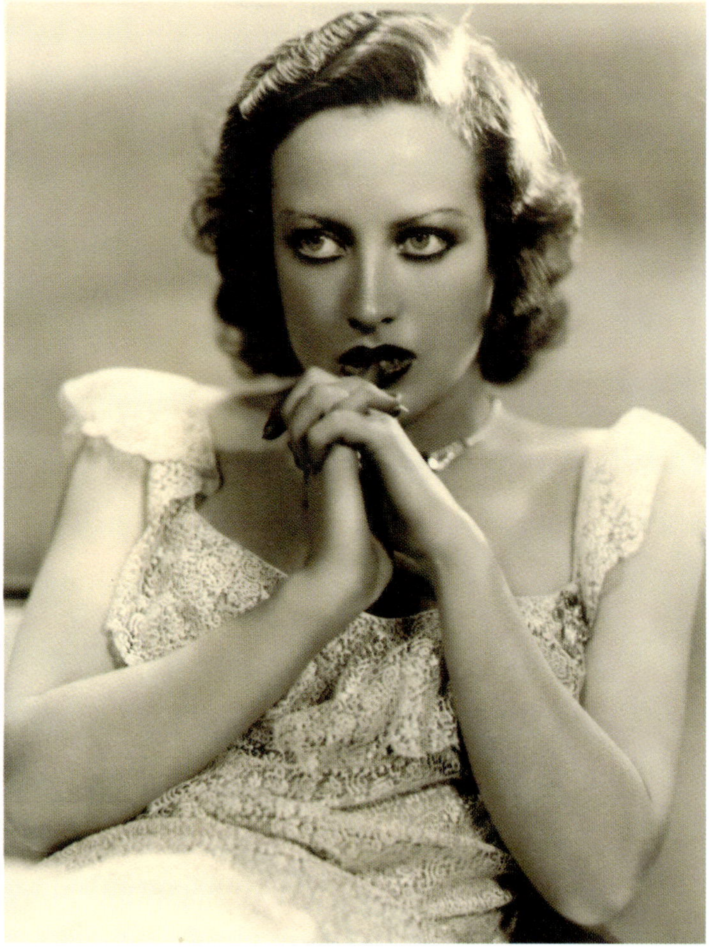

## Hurrell's Modernist Glamour Portrait

Hurrell's rapport with his subjects was distinct from Louise's, whose youth, femininity, and tact were disarming. He created sex appeal in MGM portraits—packaging what was then seen as a source of the New Woman's power (before "objectification" became a term). His dynamic physical style in the studio offended Garbo, but it relaxed and amused stars from Norma Shearer[14] (page 64) to Jean Harlow (page 21) and Ann Sheridan (page 19). With exuberant showmanship he presented the platinum blonde Harlow on a polar-bear rug and busty Jane Russell smoldering in the hay. He and Crawford collaborated with matching invention and exhibitionism in a remarkable thirty-three sittings, sessions that continued after his four-year MGM career ended (1930–33).

Hurrell built on Louise's characterization of Crawford, which took shape between 1925 and 1929 as Crawford's hair and makeup styles changed and the star as vital all-American girl

*Joan Crawford,* cat. no. 71

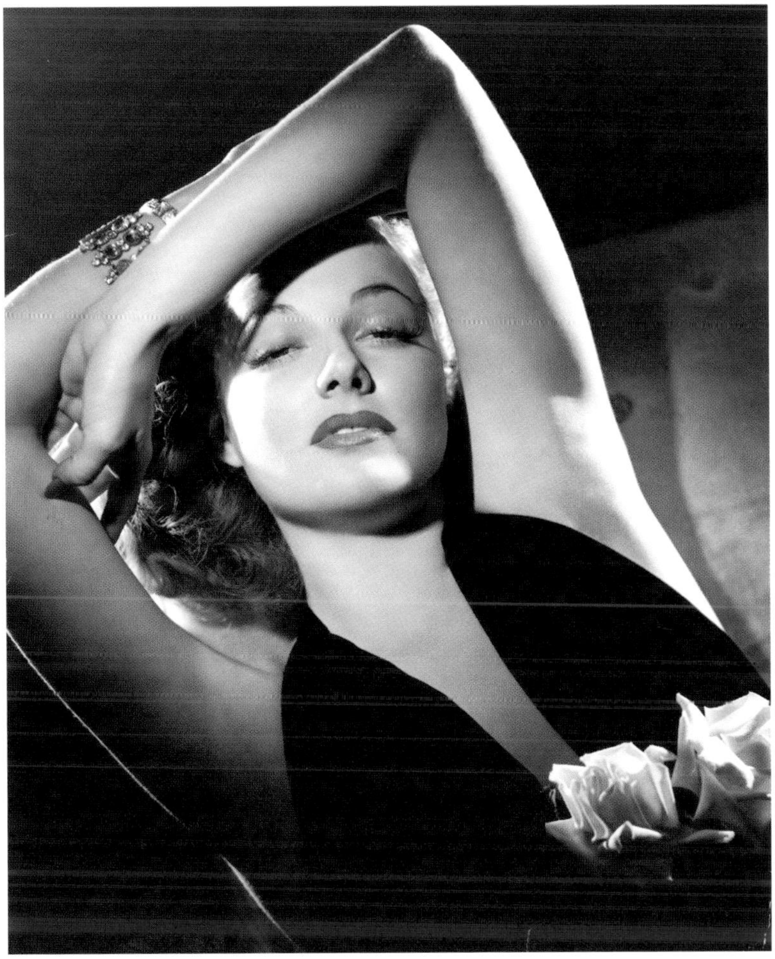

emerged and then metamorphosed into a glamorous and melodramatic New Woman and superstar (pages 18, 58, 60). Plucked from a New York chorus line, Lucille LeSueur had arrived in Hollywood some months before Garbo, but MGM announced her stardom only in 1929, months before Hurrell took Louise's position. "Crawford was a natural at posing," he said. "She had an instinctive sense of design and of herself. I photographed her literally thousands of times, and each sitting was a new experience for both of us . . . she constantly altered her appearance . . . . Yet with all the changes there was a classic beauty . . . ."[15] With Hurrell's portraits, Crawford's high energy, fashion sense, and emphatic features ("the largest eyes in Hollywood") came to define the look of the modern heroine of the '30s—assertive, independent, willing to use both sex and hard work to get ahead.

In creating that look Hurrell broke with traditional portrait techniques. While diffused lighting was used to flatter women and sharper light distinguished men, he sought "character"

*Ann Sheridan,* cat. no. 83

in both sexes through stark lighting contrasts as well as lines and details (like shadows cast by eyelashes). Custom called for three-point lighting, with the "key" light set first to establish the dominant illumination, the "fill" light set opposite it to lighten the shadows, and a back light used to separate figure from background and supplement the fill light in creating a sense of three dimensions. Hurrell, to the contrary, first set his "boom light," his adaptation of filmmaking's swooping microphone, establishing a pattern of light and shadow on face and shoulders. His key light was dimmer, and he used light bounced from reflectors or the sitter's light clothing instead of fill. Without pancake makeup, their skins gleaming, stars could rely on extensive retouching to remove blemishes (like Crawford's freckles), and darkroom work also exaggerated graphic black-and-white patterns with *noir* drama.[16]

In pursuit of variety, Hurrell tried different vantage points: from below to increase the sensual insolence of Sheridan's and Shearer's half-closed eyes; from above, to create a novel foreshortening of Crawford's marmoreal face and to accent her long-fingered hands and perfectly straight nose (page 58). The juxtaposition of modeled face and flattened dress is startling and insists on the photograph's dual identity as portrait and modernist composition.

In 1938, after five lucrative years running his own portrait studio, Hurrell joined Warner Brothers as chief portrait photographer. In this home of the gangster picture and movie musical, he adopted faster film, which let him shoot at 1/50th of a second (assuring his sitters' spontaneity with him) at f64, a small aperture for hairline clarity. He now used two boom lights to draw with illumination.[17] Ann Sheridan projects from a dark ground through a line of light around her upraised arms, her face modeled in alternating swathes of light and shadow (page 19). The Oomph Girl's expression forecasts Marilyn Monroe's in her most memorable photographs.

Such stylized images could survive in mass reproduction with its inevitable loss of detail and coarsened light-dark contrasts. Steichen also understood these limitations in magazine printing. In his lectures to advertising executives and photographers associations in the '30s, the New Yorker praised the Hollywood portraitists, while Hurrell said he subscribed to *Vogue* and *Vanity Fair* to keep up with what Steichen and Beaton were doing[18] (for example, the latter's cellophane backdrops migrated into some of Hurrell's portraits of Harlow, page 21). The two men borrowed from each other, but the crucial difference was not their creativity but their context. Hurrell served the fourth or fifth richest business in the United States, according to film magazines,[19] but it began in nickelodeons and survived on twenty-five cent tickets. Steichen, on the other hand, came from High Art.

## The Fans as Fanatics

The stars' trajectory via their images to the press and directly to their fans, to billboards, lobby cards, sheet music, film souvenir books, and the like, created the celebrity picture-saturated environment that would fascinate Pop artists. The screen goddesses as fashion ideals, both on

*Jean Harlow,* cat. no. 80

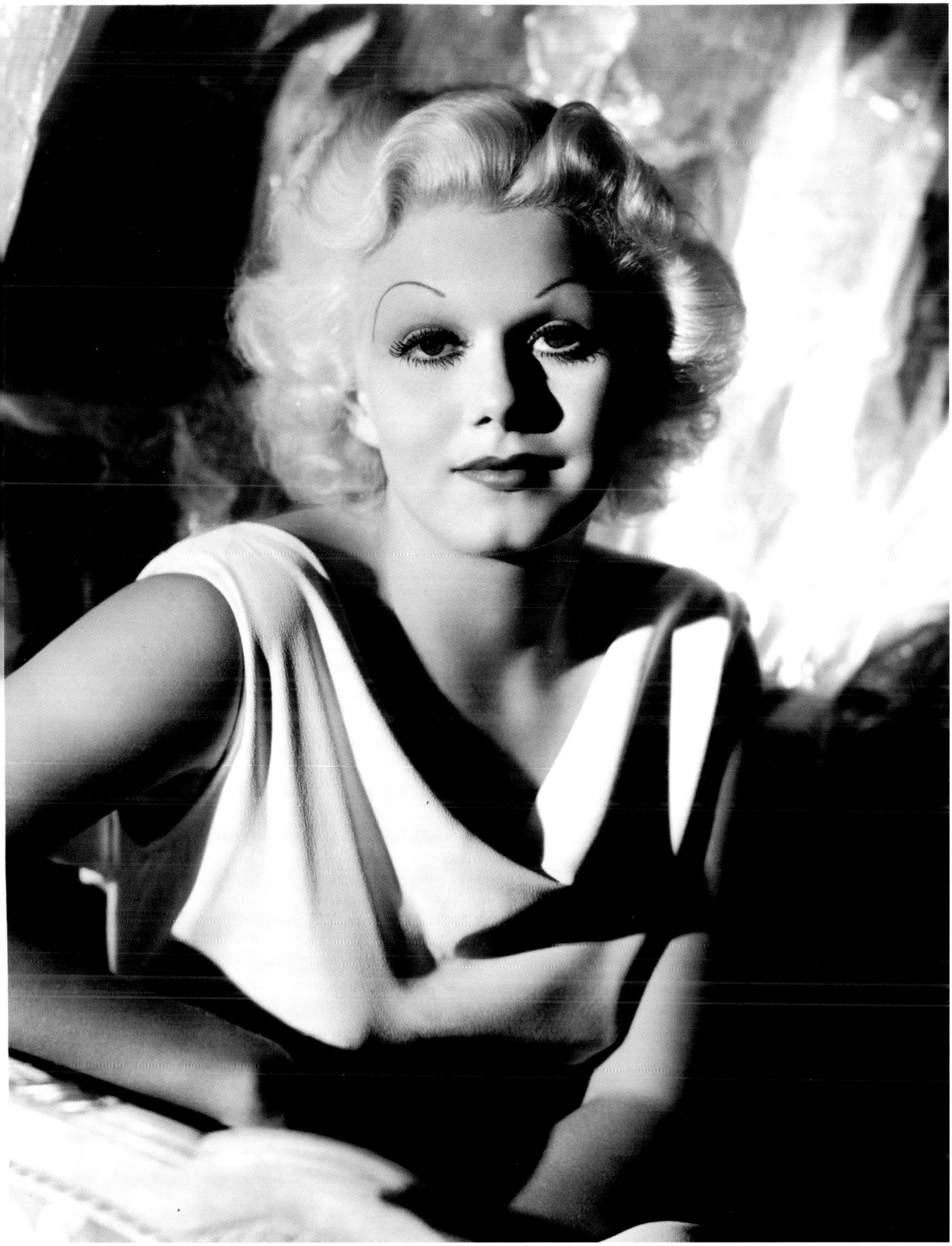

screen and off, and endorsers of goods from cosmetics to cigarettes, laid the groundwork for today's absorption with what is worn at the Oscar ceremonies and the profitable businesses of product placements in films and tie-in advertising campaigns. Fans of the '20s and '30s, however, felt a personal bond with Hollywood that went far beyond their weekly consumption of films.

The fan-star bond was cemented by the free photographs signed by their favorites (the 4 x 5-inch prints sent with a penny stamp)[20] and the fan clubs fostered by the movie magazines. Contests for "signed and framed photos of the stars" could be entered with a coupon from a monthly and a hundred-word description of the "beloved" one. The dozens of prizewinners were announced in the next issue. The studios' casting books were combined and reproduced as filmdom yearbooks by *Photoplay,* for example, and offered as premiums with subscriptions. In all these photo-reproductions, the stars remained glamorous, and, paradoxically, their lives seemed just within reach. Especially in the Depression years, an attractive girl yearned to be "discovered" at a soda fountain like Lana Turner. In otherwise anonymous urban life, she found exciting social rituals and group identity in movie-going and fan clubs. The next set of photographs she received led her to the silver screen and made her feel her opinion mattered. And it did, as Hollywood monitored its ticket sales and fan mail.

## The End

The photojournalist as prying paparazzo (*mosquito* in an Italian dialect) got his name from Federico Fellini's *La Dolce Vita* (1960), which could be said to mark the fadeout for Hollywood's Golden Age and its glamour portraits. Fellini's sensationalist photographer pursues bodacious Anita Ekberg across Rome (Figure 3) but also hounds a literary hero's wife about to be told of his suicide. Their media-wise world is just a few years away from Andy Warhol's, where everyone, the Pop artist promised, would be famous for fifteen minutes. Fellini's film itself was celebrated as part of the New Wave of European cinema, in which the director's individual vision and the cinematographer's rule-breaking invention would challenge the formulas of big-studio American pictures.

Also in Rome at the time, Elizabeth Taylor filmed *Cleopatra* with Richard Burton, and their off-screen romance sparked more coverage than the extravagant film itself. "The most beautiful woman in the world" was playing the ancient world's most scandalous one and relishing her privileges, notwithstanding her fourth marriage and Burton's first one. With a superstar's command of her image, however, the actress went on to further notoriety but also fame, including two acting Oscars, and she made front-page news when she died at age seventy-nine.

Taylor is ravishing in the '60s and '70s stills and portraits that Robert Dance has collected (pages 66, 68, 69, 70); he views her as the last of the studio system's goddesses. She witnessed the end of epic costume films and the rise of independent "brat pack" filmmakers, and in later years she used her still-magnetic celebrity to raise funds for AIDS research. Film and photography

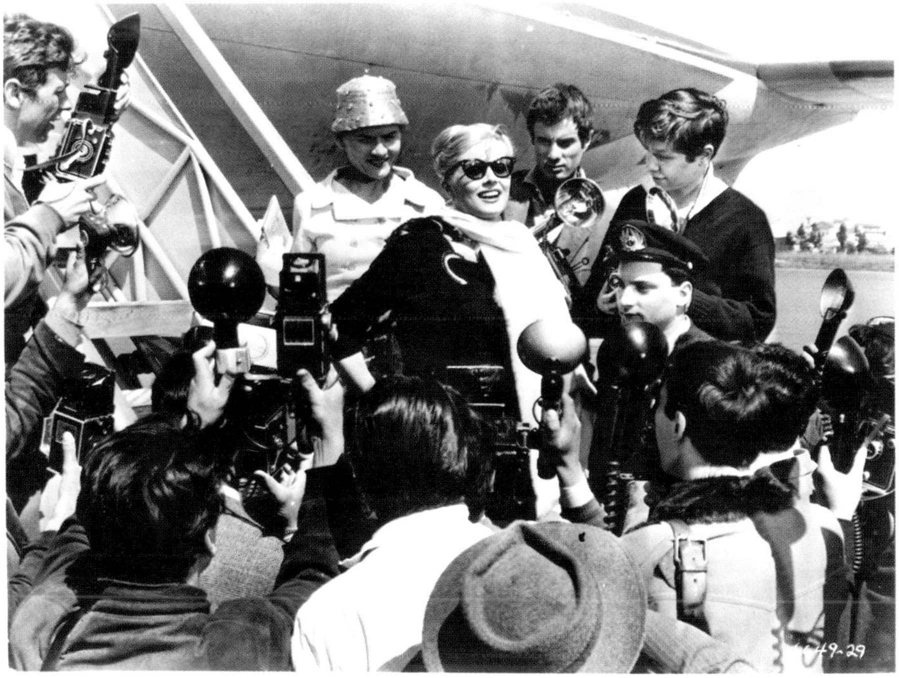

vogues had changed. As aging star Norma Desmond (Gloria Swanson) sneered about her fallen fortunes in *Sunset Boulevard* (1950), "I AM big. It's the pictures that got small."

Tastes had evolved after World War II and the glamour portrait began to fade in part through the very magazines that had promoted it. The strong suit of *Life* and the other mid-century pictorial magazines was 35mm photojournalism, caught on the streets, not staged in the studio before view cameras. And the verism of war coverage, paralleled in postwar Neo-Realism in Italian cinema, enhanced respect for a more candid language. Erich Salomon's *Celebrated Contemporaries in Unguarded Moments* had been published in 1931, and Weegee's flash-bombed grab shots of mobster rub-outs and hookers in paddy wagons sold tabloids in the '30s and '40s. This defiant side in photo consumption was strengthened in the '50s and '60s by Beat and counterculture rejections of traditional norms of beauty and institutional authority.

Today the link between photography and fame is most striking in "reality TV" and the stunts of "real" people as recorded by video cameras and cell phones and transmitted globally. Fame may be measured not in minutes but seconds. The Hollywood glamour portrait survives in photo-history, however, to remind us of a different, asymmetrical relation between the viewer and beauty, fame, and photography. The Dance collection demonstrates that such camera alchemy—from the disappearing world of gelatin silver film—can still trigger memory and thought.

FIGURE 3 (above) Pier Luigi, *Anita Ekberg and the paparazzi* in La Dolce Vita, 1960.

## Notes

1 Louise Brooks, as quoted in John Kobal, *The Art of the Great Hollywood Photographers* (New York: Knopf, 1980), 122.

2 DVC, "Catching the Highlights," *New York Times,* September 6, 1936, quoted in Robert Dance, *Glamour of the Gods* (London and New York: Rizzoli, 2010), 21.

3 Consolidated from many smaller companies by around 1925, "the Big Five" were Metro-Goldwyn-Mayer, Warner Brothers, RKO-Radio, Paramount, and Fox.

4 Regarding on-set relations, Garbo's successful demand for William Daniels as her cinematographer was exceptional, as was the collaboration between Dietrich and director Josef von Sternberg in the creation of her still image.

5 Kobal, *Great Hollywood Photographers*, 79.

6 This information derives from Robert Hudovernik, *Jazz Age Beauties: The Lost Collection of Ziegfeld Photographer Alfred Cheney Johnston* (New York: Universe, 2006).

7 The portrait was reproduced full-page, November 12, 1925, p. 80: see ill. in Robin Muir, *The World's Most Photographed* (London: National Portrait Gallery, 2006), 73.

8 For the best example, see Robert Dance and Bruce Robertson, *Ruth Harriet Louise and Hollywood Glamour Photography* (Berkeley, Los Angeles, London: University of California Press in association with the Santa Barbara Museum of Art, 2002) , repro. opp. p. 1.

9 Ibid., 176.

10 Ibid., 179.

11 For a thorough investigation, see Patricia Johnston, *Real Fantasies: Edward Steichen's Advertising Photography* (Berkeley and Los Angeles: University of California Press, 1997).

12 Fan and camera magazines profiled studio photographers from time to time, but their cultural standing was far from that of *Vanity Fair* and *Vogue*. For his part, Steichen had received art world attention for his Pictorialist photography and painting in the early 1900s, whereas Hollywood's interwar glamour portraits were exhibited as an important photographic genre only in the 1970s: note the Victoria & Albert's pioneering exhibition in 1974 of selections from the John Kobal collection, which generated his 1980 book *The Art of the Great Hollywood Photographers*.

13 That their styles were recognizable is the point of an April 1933 *Vanity Fair* illustration by George Hoyningen-Huene in which Mme. Lucien Lelong poses in the styles of these and three other photographers (reproduced in Johnston, *Real Fantasies*, 7. 25). The anonymous caption writer concluded, "Does the style of the photographer obliterate the personality of the sitter? Is photography Art?"

14 Ramon Novarro recommended Hurrell to Shearer in 1929 when she wanted to convince her husband, MGM production chief Irving Thalberg, that she could play the "bad girl" roles given to Garbo and Crawford. Hurrell's steamy portrayal of the elegant actress won her *The Divorcée* and won him the portrait phtographer's job at MGM. See pp. 7–10 in the first significant study of Hurrell, Whitney Stines's *50 Years of Photograping Hollywood: The Hurrell Style* (New York: John Day Company, 1976).

15 Ibid., 62. Stines's quotation from Hurrell is embellished in Mark A. Vieira, *Hurrell's Hollywood Portraits: The Chapman Collection* (New York: Abrams, 1997), 50.

16 Ibid., 50–51.

17 Ibid., 51.

18 Ibid., 105.

19 *Picture Play* reported in July 1916 that "movies are the fifth largest business in the United States," with 18,000 theaters across the country (quoted in Kobal, *Great Hollywood Photographers,* 46). In "the World's Latest Fine Art," *Cinema Arts*, June 1937, n.p., Rouben Mamoulian stated that films are the "4th largest industry in the world," and there are 36,000 theaters in the United States.

20 During Crawford's nearly twenty years at MGM, the studio paid postage for mailing her portraits (from small to 8 x 10-inch) to fans; requests averaged five thousand a month. Later, after her contract ended, she continued to send out prints and paid the postage herself. See Terence Pepper and John Kobal, *The Man Who Shot Garbo: The Hollywood Photographs of Clarence Sinclair Bull* (New York: Simon & Schuster, 1989), 235.

# Silver Screen ✷ Silver Prints

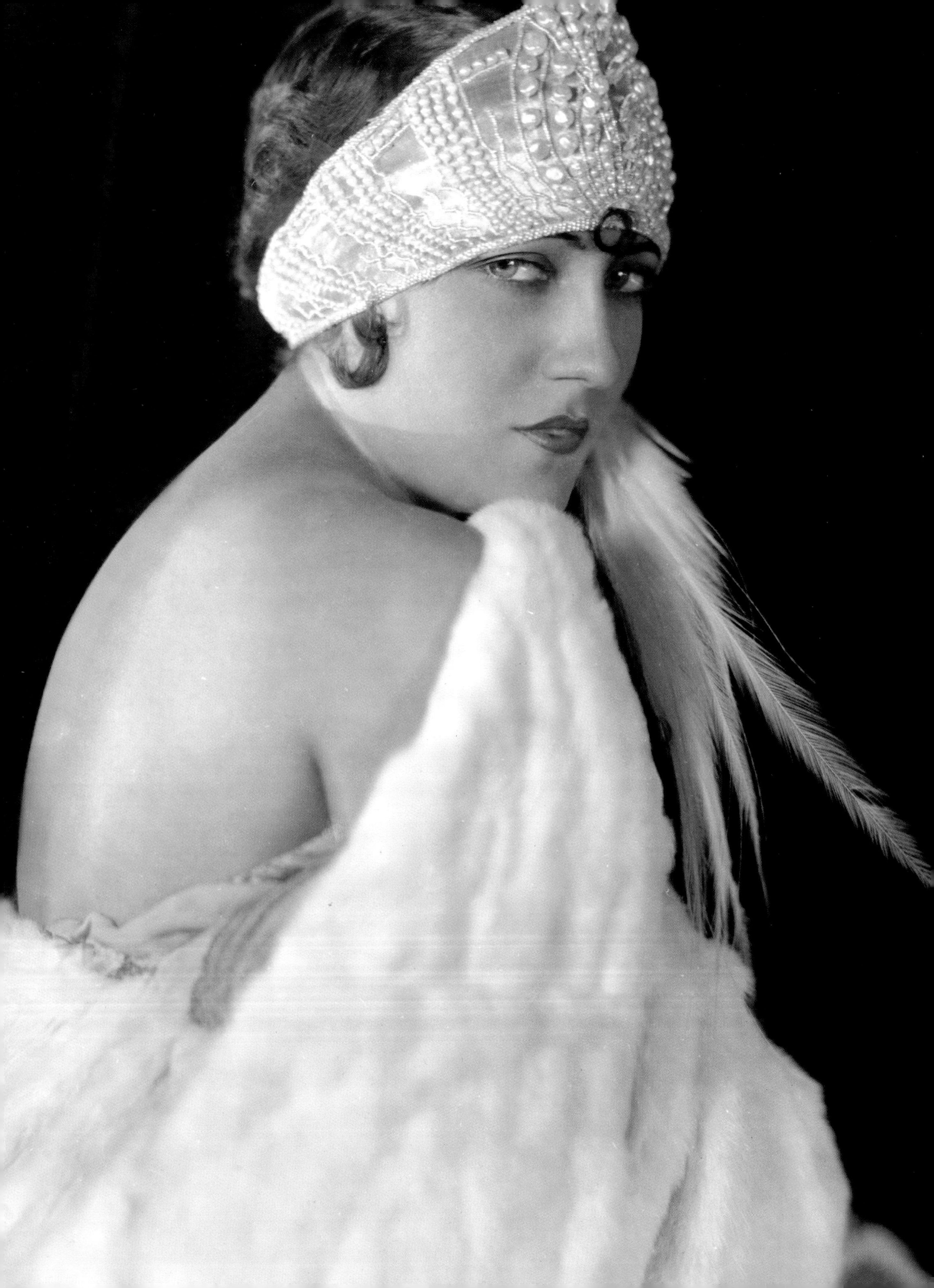

# Independent Photographers

Before the advent of the Hollywood studio system in the mid-1920s, which brought all components of filmmaking and publicity under the aegis of each major company, screen actors and actresses were largely responsible for promoting their own images. Stars and featured players hired independent photographers, provided portraits to their directors and producers, and sent them to fans. Most photographers for the film industry operated from New York or Los Angeles. One notable exception was Strauss-Peyton Studios of Kansas City. Nearly every important stage, screen, or vaudeville star of the teens and early 1920s stopped by to be photographed—including Gloria Swanson, who apparently traveled with her best jewels and furs.

James Abbe (1883–1973) was among the most prominent photographers of silent film performers. He opened his studio in New York around 1917, but was frequently in Los Angeles or Paris following his famous clients, such as the Gish sisters, Rudolph Valentino, Mary Pickford, and Douglas Fairbanks. Another notable photographer of the mid-1920s was Arthur Rice, who boasted Rudolph Valentino as a client. He photographed "the Latin Lover" and his co-star Alla Nazimova for *Camille* (1921), and portrayed Nazimova again when she made *Salome* the following year. Russell Ball (c. 1894–1942) began his career in New York before moving to Los Angeles in 1926, and was a favorite of glamour queens such as Gloria Swanson.

The leading New York theatrical photographer, Alfred Cheney Johnston (1884–1971) specialized in risqué renderings of the Ziegfeld Girls. Mae Murray, dubbed "the girl with the bee-stung lips," was one of them, and like Ziegfeld's discoveries Louise Brooks and Marion Davies, she went on to become a Hollywood star.

From the start, film industry photographers observed a pecking order. At the top were the portrait artists in their private studios. Only the most important project, producer, or director could woo them onto film sets. Secondary photographers were hired principally to shoot scene stills and general publicity photographs: they worked on a film-to-film basis. Some directors used the same photographer time and again, notably the comic genius Mack Sennett who chose George Cannons to shoot the saucy starlets in his slapstick comedies.

Stars too had their favorites, and Albert W. Witzel (1879–1929) was among the earliest photographers to cater to them. He made the most alluring photographs of Theda Bara, a silent film siren who was probably the first movie star in the modern sense of the word. Like the silents themselves, early portrait photographs for films—often of half or full length figures—drew on the conventions of high art, theater, and vaudeville.

*Gloria Swanson,* cat. no. 3

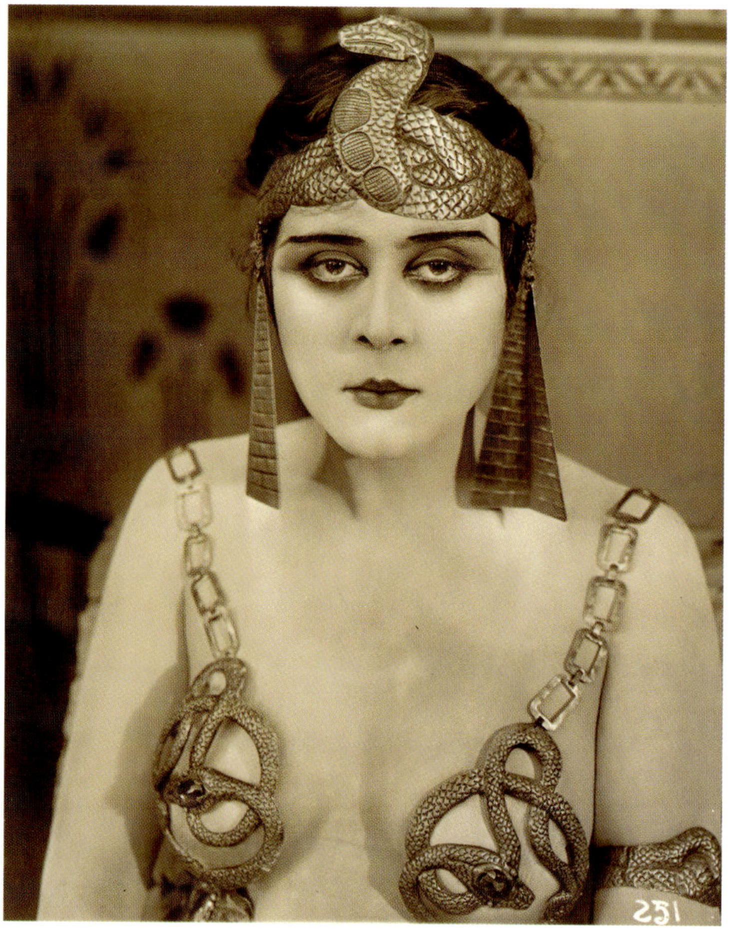

1 Albert Witzel, *Theda Bara,* 1917, for *Cleopatra,* gelatin silver print, 10 x 8 inches

2 Alfred Cheney Johnston (New York), *Mae Murray,* c. 1920, gelatin silver print, 14 x 11 inches

3 Strauss-Peyton Studio (Kansas City), *Gloria Swanson,* 1922, gelatin silver print, 14 x 11 inches

4 Arthur Rice, *Alla Nazimova,* 1922, for *Salome,* gelatin silver print, 10 x 8 inches

5 George Cannons, *Thelma Parr,* c. 1925, for Mack Sennett Comedies, gelatin silver print, 10 x 8 inches

6 Russell Ball, *Gloria Swanson,* c. 1925, gelatin silver print, 14 x 11 inches

7 James Abbe (Paris), *Mary Pickford and Douglas Fairbanks,* 1925, gelatin silver print, 13 x 10 inches

8 Albert Witzel, *Dorothy Revier,* 1927, for *The Clown,* gelatin silver print, 14 x 11 inches

*Theda Bara* (above), cat. no. 1
*Alla Nazimova* (opposite), cat. no. 4

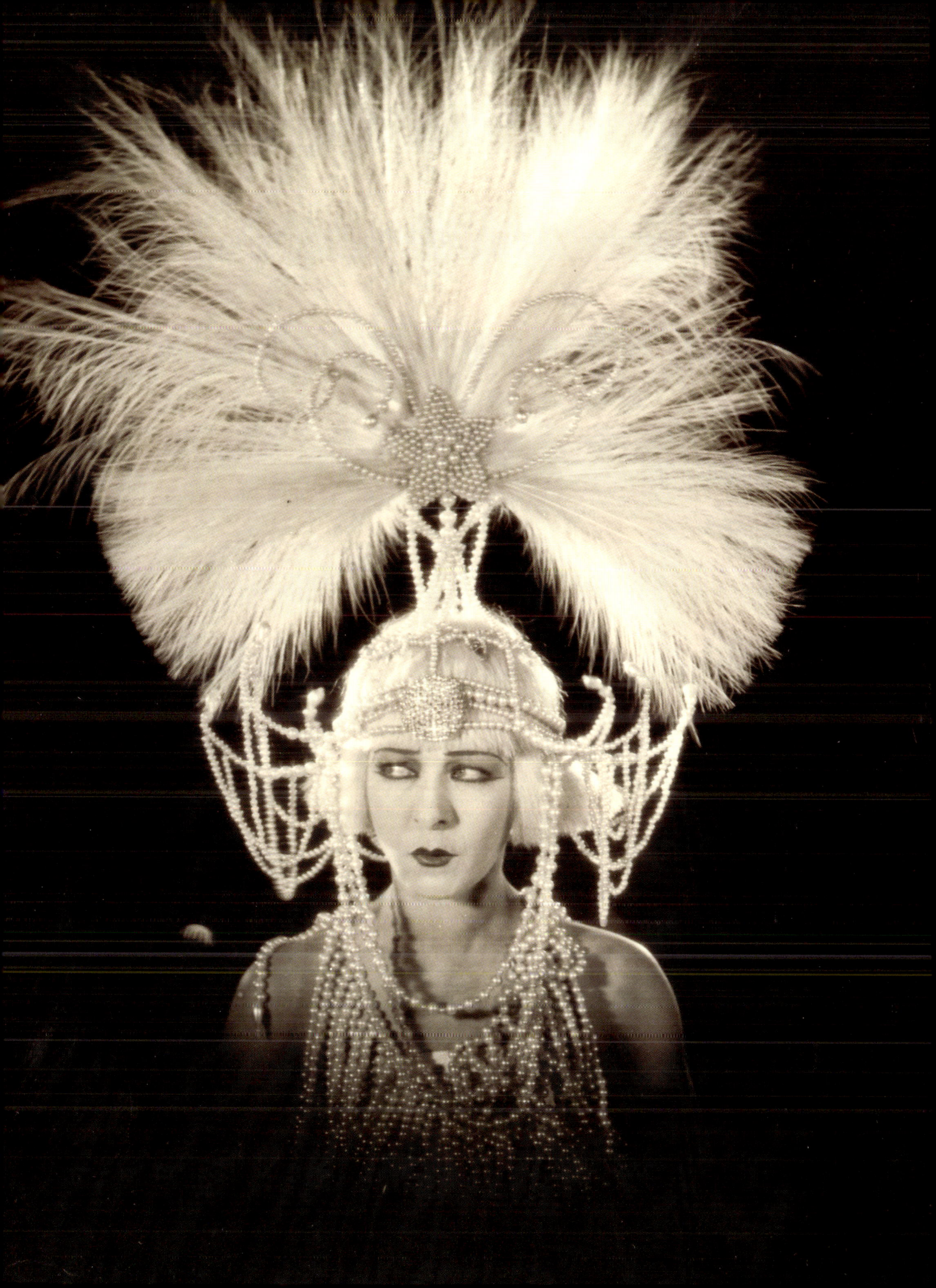

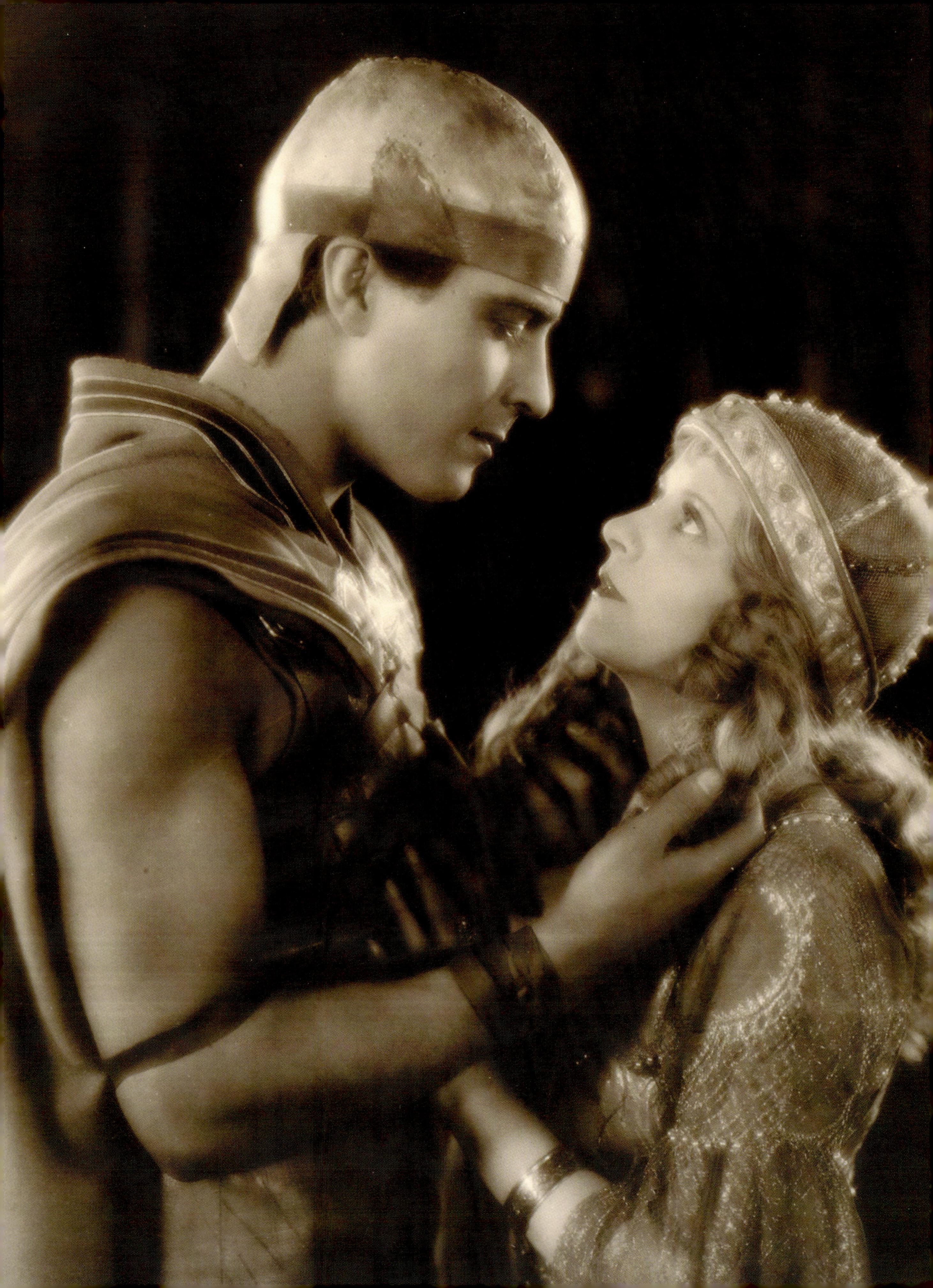

# Ramon Novarro

Mexican-born Ramon Novarro (1899–1968) was among Hollywood's first generation of dashing young Latin superstars. Rudolph Valentino, four years Novarro's senior, defined the romantic category with his great success starring in the *Four Horsemen of the Apocalypse* (1921), a film in which Novarro played a bit part. The next year Novarro became a leading man in his own right with his performance in *The Prisoner of Zenda*. Valentino epitomized this exotic type for the next few years until Novarro appeared as the title character in MGM's 1925 epic *Ben-Hur*. This role established Novarro as the nation's heart throb at the moment Valentino's star was beginning to wane. The latter's sudden death in 1926 put Novarro on top, and his only rival in romance was John Gilbert, Greta Garbo's on- and off-screen lover. Gilbert played the handsome all-American type while Novarro exuded continental sophistication and charm.

Novarro was a photographer's dream subject. Handsome and at ease before the portrait camera, he could portray any mood convincingly, from serious to playful. He was the first male star to be photographed with the same sense of Eros found in photographs of women, and his delight in being photographed set him apart from other male stars such as Gilbert, Douglas Fairbanks, and even Valentino, all of whom look much better in motion on the screen than frozen in portraits. Not so Novarro. Like his great leading ladies Joan Crawford and Greta Garbo, he was as compelling a portrait subject as a film personality.

This was first revealed in the extensive portrait and still photography made for *Ben-Hur*. Working with many different photographers first in Europe and later in America over the two years it took to make the film, Novarro gamely posed for pictures clad in military attire, Roman togas, and sometimes nothing more than a loincloth.

Novarro's silent films after *Ben-Hur* confirmed his star status and he was a consistent money-maker for his studio. When sound came to the movies he made the transition effortlessly, and it turned out he had a good singing voice so he was often cast in musicals. His best-known talkie is the drama *Mata Hari* (1931), in which he co-starred with Garbo. Nevertheless, with the advent of sound and the hard times of the Depression, the era of the Latin lover came to an end and male stars of the rugged masculine variety such as Clark Gable and James Cagney became popular favorites. Novarro stayed at MGM for a decade after making *Ben-Hur,* but by 1935 his kinds of films were no longer finding an audience. Fortune and reputation secure, Novarro left MGM in 1935 and only worked occasionally. In the 1940s and 1950s he took on interesting character roles in films such as *The Big Steal* (1949) and *The Outriders* (1950).

*Ramon Novarro and May McAvoy,* cat. no. 13

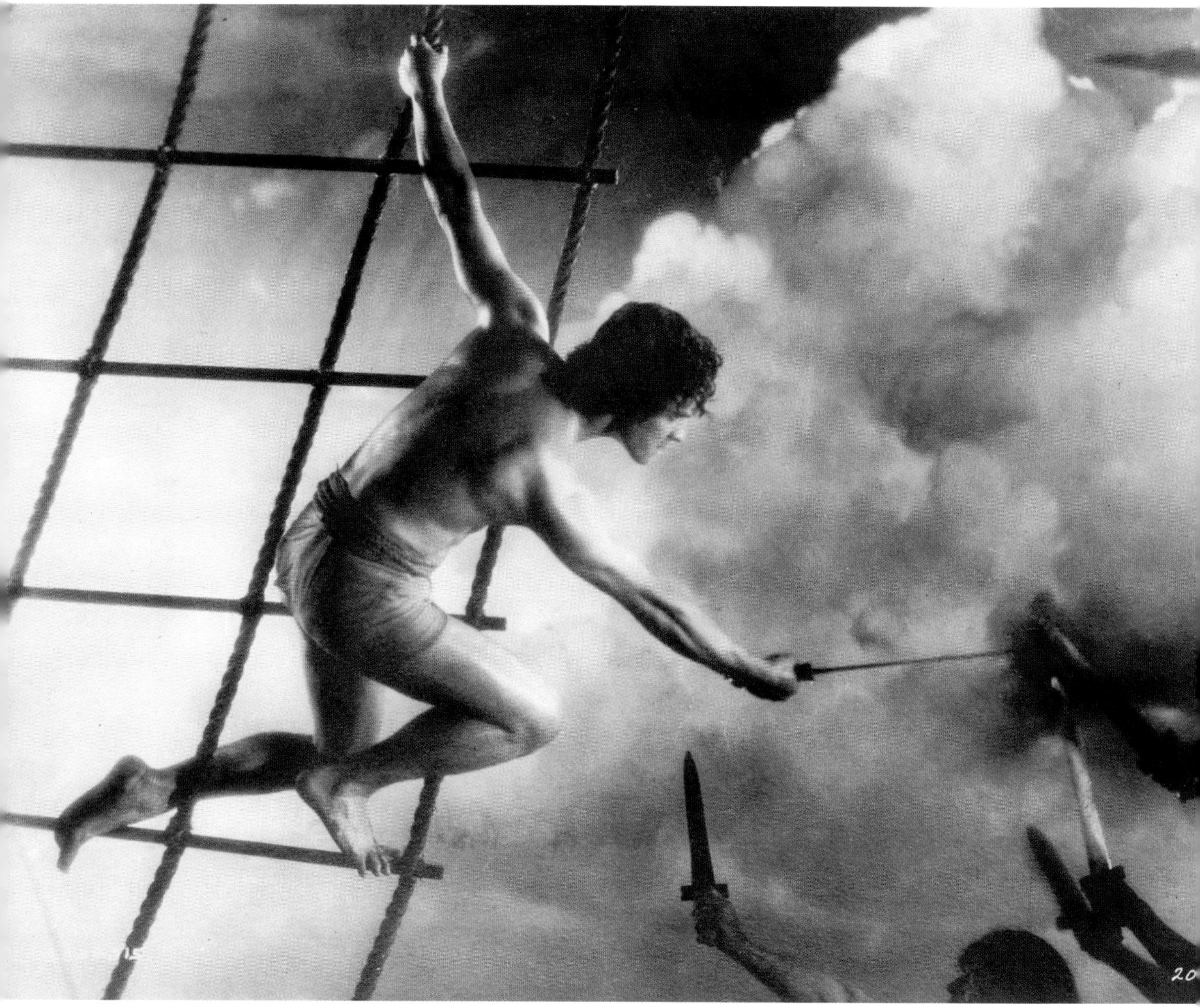

*Ramon Novarro* (above), cat. no. 10
*Ramon Novarro* (opposite), cat. no. 15

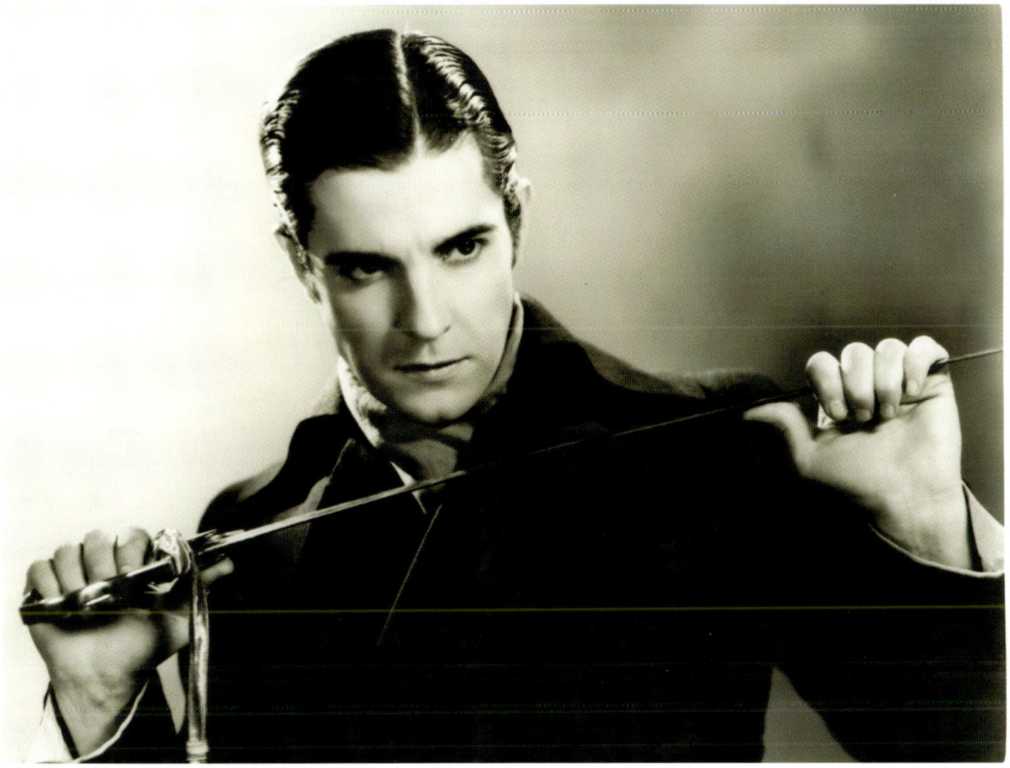

9 [Photographer unknown], *Ramon Novarro,* 1924, for *The Arab,* gelatin silver print, 10 x 8 inches

10 Henry Lachman, *Ramon Novarro,* 1925, for *Ben-Hur*, gelatin silver print, 10 x 13 inches

11 [Photographer unknown], *Ramon Novarro and Francis X. Bushman,* 1925, for *Ben-Hur,* gelatin silver print, 10 x 13 inches

12 [Photographer unknown], *Ramon Novarro and galley slaves,* 1925, for *Ben-Hur*, gelatin silver print, 10 x 13 inches

13 Warren Lynch (attributed to), *Ramon Novarro and May McAvoy,* 1925, for *Ben-Hur*, gelatin silver print, 13 x 10 inches

14 Ruth Harriet Louise, *Ramon Novarro and Jean Hersholt,* 1927, for *The Student Prince in Old Heidelberg,* gelatin silver print, 10 x 13 inches

15 Clarence Sinclair Bull, *Ramon Novarro,* 1929, for *Devil May Care,* gelatin silver print, 10 x 13 inches

16 Milton Brown, *Ramon Novarro and Greta Garbo,* 1931, for *Mata Hari,* gelatin silver print, 13 x 10 inches

17 Carl van Vechten (New York), *Ramon Novarro,* April 3, 1934, gelatin silver print, 14 x 11 inches

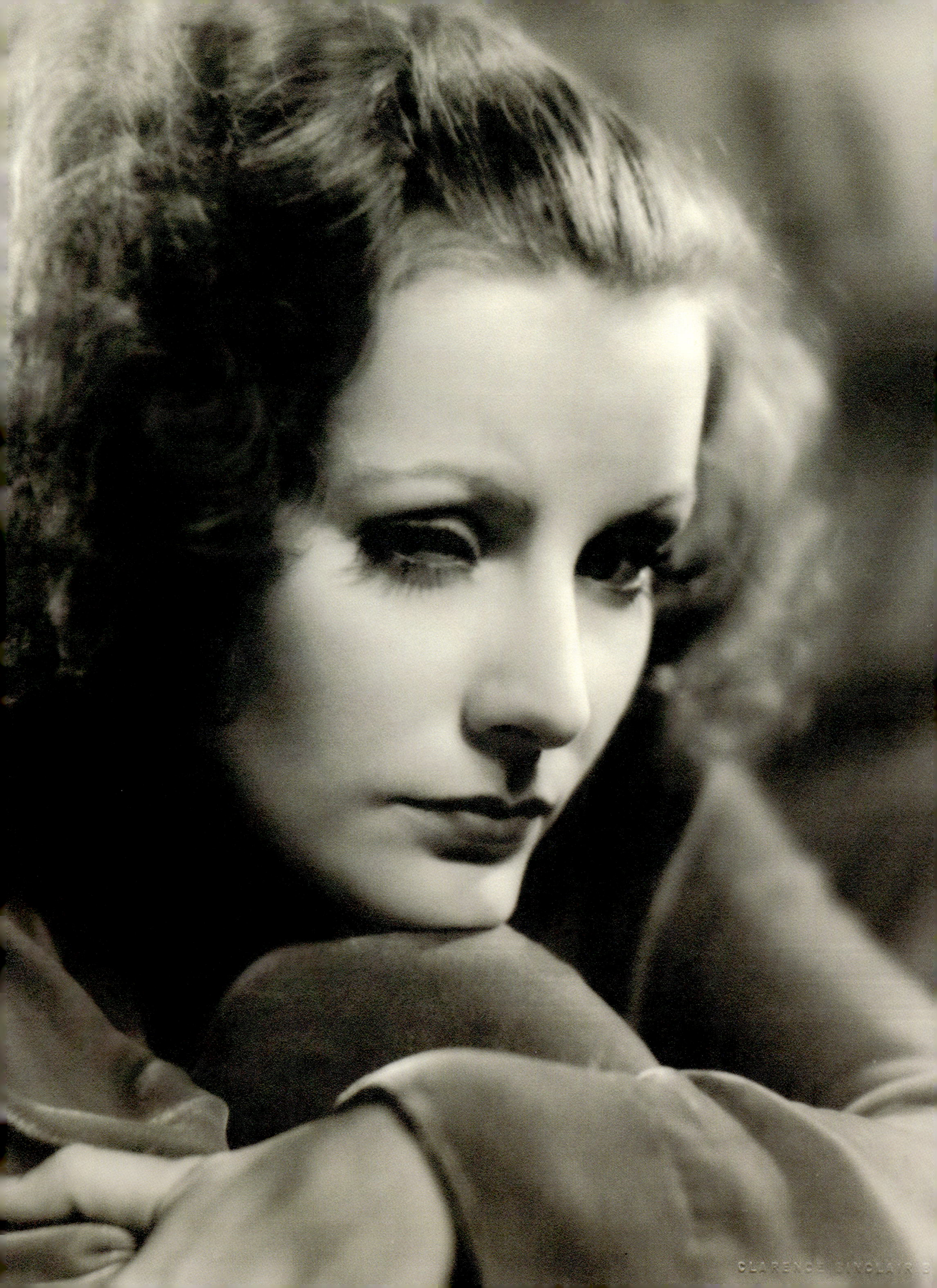

# Garbo

Greta Garbo (1905–1990) was Hollywood's epitome of glamour and beauty and arguably the screen's finest dramatic actress between the wars. None of this was foreordained. The nineteen-year-old who crossed the Atlantic from her native Sweden in the summer of 1925 with an MGM contract was met at the New York docks by a lone free-lance photographer hired by the studio to document her arrival. The pictures taken that July day depict a pretty, simply attired Hollywood hopeful not unlike thousands of others with dreams of movie stardom. This would soon change.

Garbo was photographed twice during the summer months she spent in New York before heading to Los Angeles. The first time was under MGM's auspices but the photographs were not memorable. Garbo as a thrilling portrait subject was first revealed when she sat for Arnold Genthe in late July 1925. From Genthe she learned that acting was not reserved for the film set, but that similar effort and emotion could be directed to the portrait camera, and with spectacular results.

Ruth Harriet Louise, chief portrait photographer at MGM, made Garbo's first Hollywood portraits in September 1925. The portrait from that initial session marks the beginning of a remarkable collaboration between artist and subject, one producing the face that enthralled movie-goers. During the months while Garbo made her first American film, *Torrent* (1926), the curly hair yielded to a sleek shoulder-length cut and she lost weight. The supreme love goddess of the movies was born.

After Louise's departure from MGM in late 1929, Clarence Sinclair Bull became Garbo's principal photographer. For the next twelve years, Bull would control, with few exceptions, the image that her studio presented to the public. At the completion of each film they met for a single day-long session. Between sixty and a hundred negatives would be exposed depending largely on the number of costume changes Garbo needed to make. Although the diva had absolute veto over her portraits, she rarely rejected one of Bull's negatives.

Clarence Bull only slightly refined Ruth Harriet Louise's earlier work. Hollywood's biggest star was well known to her public. MGM decreed there would be no change to the Garbo image. Bull's task was to update the Garbo portrait continually but without fundamentally altering her persona. With a sharper focus and more extreme close-ups in the 1930s, he dramatized Garbo's beauty magnificently. Collaborations with an actress who fully understood the power of the portrait, Bull's photographs of Garbo have become icons of Hollywood imagery.

*Greta Garbo,* cat. no. 22

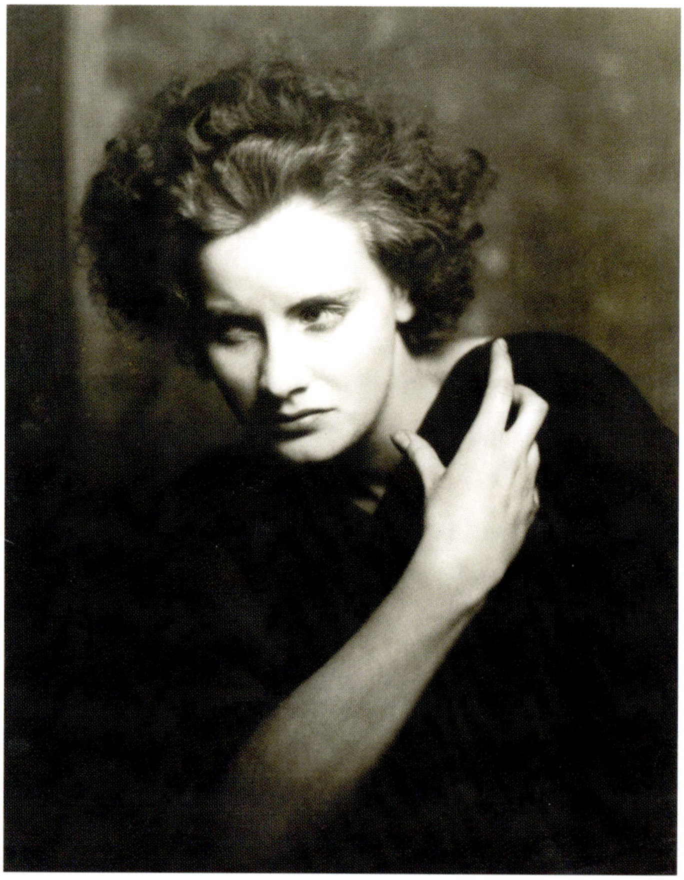

18 Arnold Genthe (New York), *Greta Garbo,* 1925, gelatin silver print, 13 x 10 inches

19 Ruth Harriet Louise, *Greta Garbo,* 1925, for *Torrent,* gelatin silver print, 10 x 8 inches

20 Ruth Harriet Louise, *Greta Garbo,* 1927, for *Divine Woman,* gelatin silver print, 13 x 10 inches

21 William Grimes, *Greta Garbo and John Gilbert,* 1927, for *Love,* gelatin silver print, 10 x 13 inches

22 Clarence Sinclair Bull, *Greta Garbo,* 1931, for *Inspiration,* gelatin silver print, 13 x 10 inches

23 Clarence Sinclair Bull, *Greta Garbo,* 1931, for *Mata Hari,* gelatin silver print, 13 x 10 inches

24 Clarence Sinclair Bull, *Greta Garbo,* 1931, for *Grand Hotel,* gelatin silver print, 13 x 10 inches

25 Clarence Sinclair Bull, *Greta Garbo,* 1933, for *Queen Christina,* gelatin silver print, 13 x 10 inches

26 Clarence Sinclair Bull, *Greta Garbo,* 1939, for *Ninotchka,* gelatin silver print, 13 x 10 inches

27 Clarence Sinclair Bull, *Greta Garbo,* 1939, for *Ninotchka,* gelatin silver print, 13 x 10 inches

*Greta Garbo* (above), cat. no. 18
*Greta Garbo* (opposite), cat. no. 23

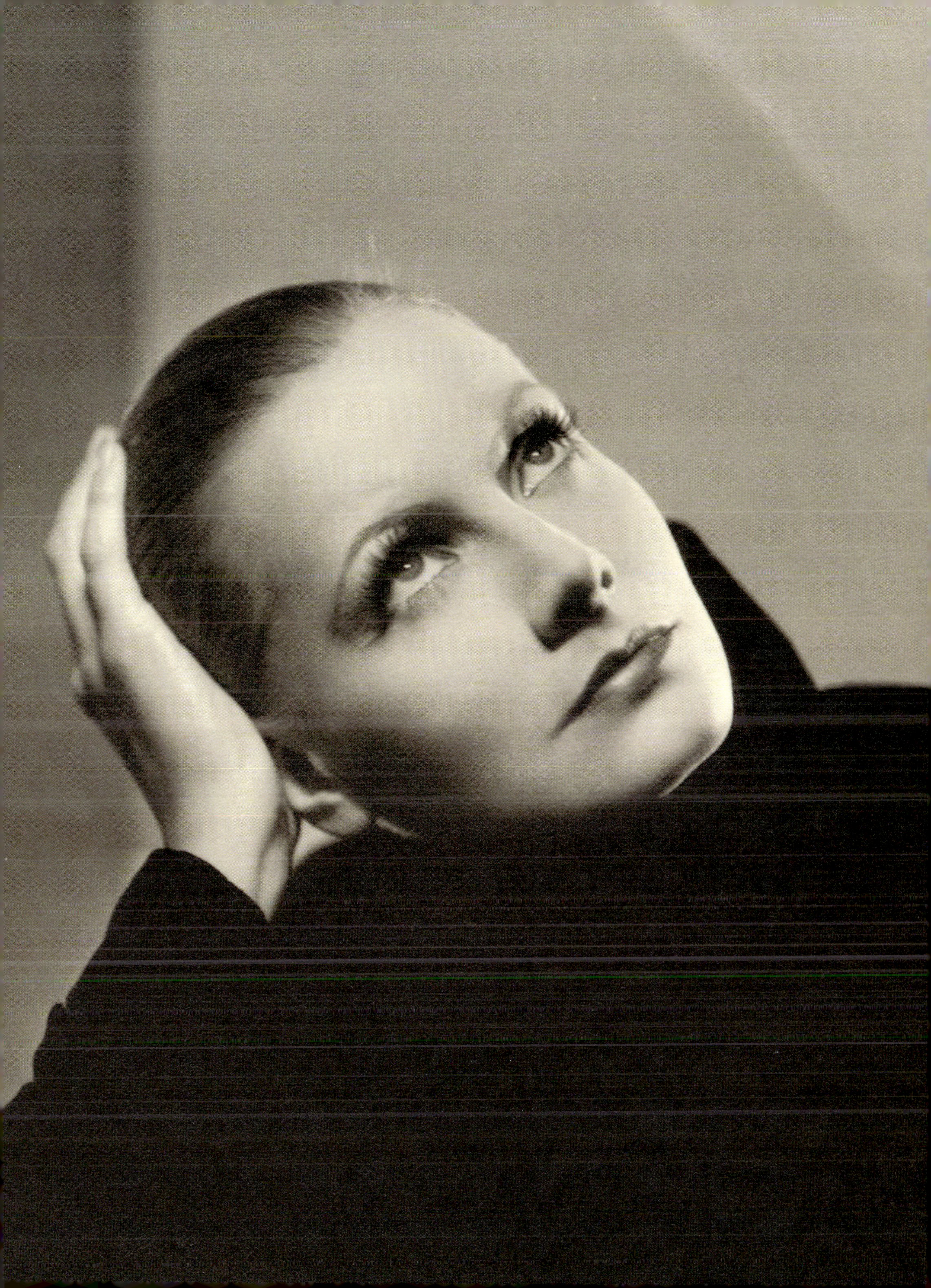

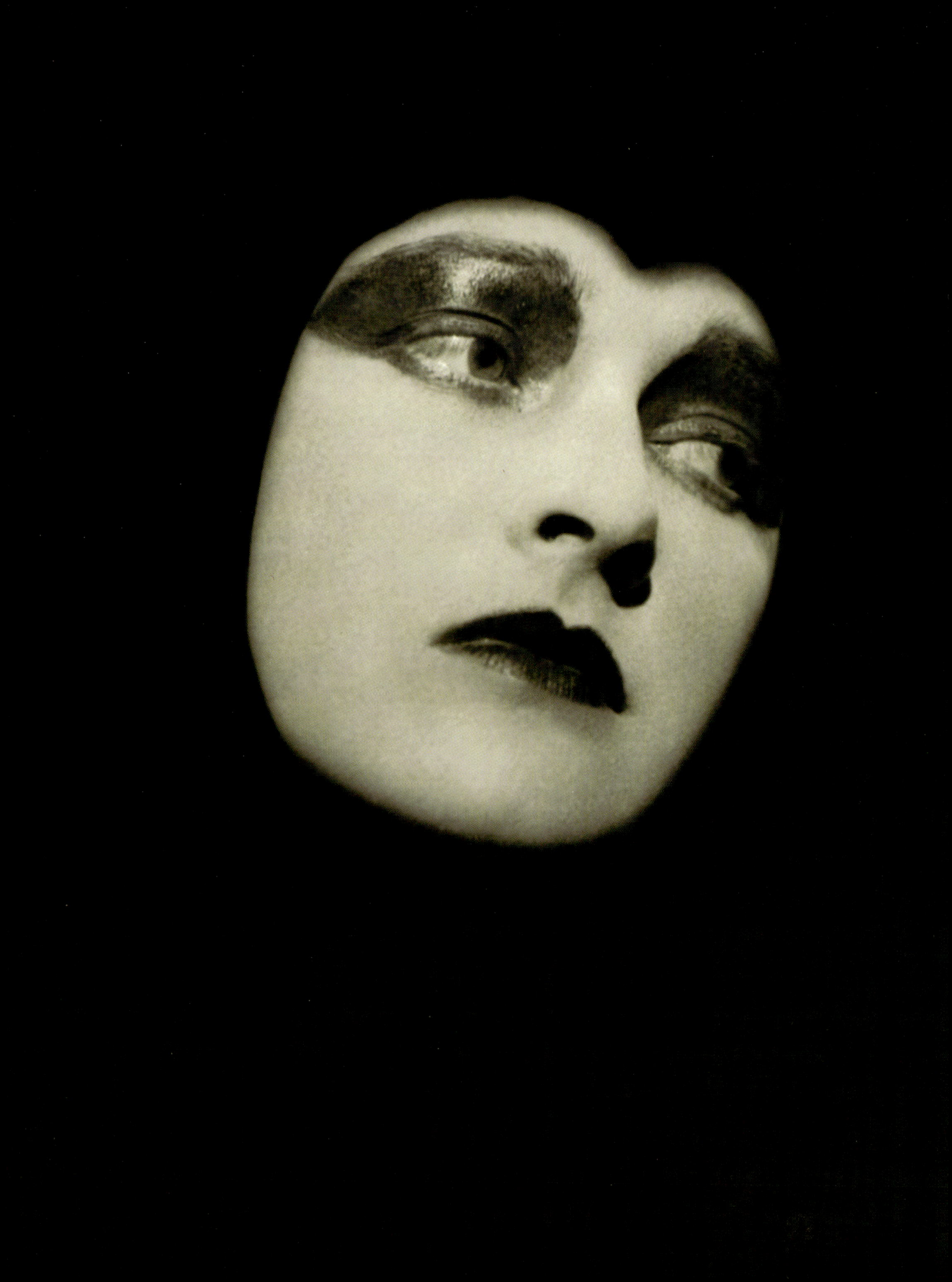

# Ruth Harriet Louise

Talent, timing, connections, and youth combined to give Ruth Harriet Louise (1903–1940) unprecedented power in helping to create the Hollywood glamour portrait. Born Ruth Goldstein in New York, the daughter of a rabbi, she took up photography as a girl and after finishing high school she trained with society favorite Nickolas Muray. He introduced her to the portrait devices of East Coast sophisticates. Her professionalism in her own studio led her first cousin Carmel Myers, one of filmdom's reigning sirens, to encourage her to move her business to Hollywood. Louise's brother had already moved there and set the path that would later make him a director of Fred Astaire and Ginger Rogers's best musicals. In spring 1925 in Hollywood, Louise was introduced to MGM's head of publicity, and after a trial of a few months she was named the studio's chief portrait photographer. The lone woman to head a portrait gallery at any studio during Hollywood's glory years, she was twenty-two.

Louise could work with current soft-focus Pictorialist conventions, and she knew how to highlight attractive physical features and to add an artful gesture of the hands or a slight turn of the head or upper torso. But she was also a forerunner in seeking to reveal something of her sitter's character—whether an actual personality or a role enacted on the screen—and she used her feminine charm and youth to draw out her subjects. Starlets, who were often close to her in age, enjoyed posing for her, and she could create silly pictures that were often picked up by the fan magazines. The fun-loving Marion Davies was a favorite subject, and the two New Yorkers often had sessions outside the studio—a rarity for studio portraitists. At the opposite extreme, Louise experimented with new formal devices, such as the "mask" portrait of actress Eleanor Boardman. In her studio, their favorite music playing on her Victrola, performers seemed to relax and they participated effectively in the creative process of studio portraiture—a contractual obligation that not every performer enjoyed fulfilling.

Louise served female stars best during her MGM career, 1925–29, and later in her free-lance years. She is as responsible for creating the glamorous images of Greta Garbo and Joan Crawford as any of their cinematographers or directors—Garbo luminous and swooning for love, Crawford alive with high-voltage energy.

*Mask Photograph (Eleanor Boardman)*, cat. no. 35

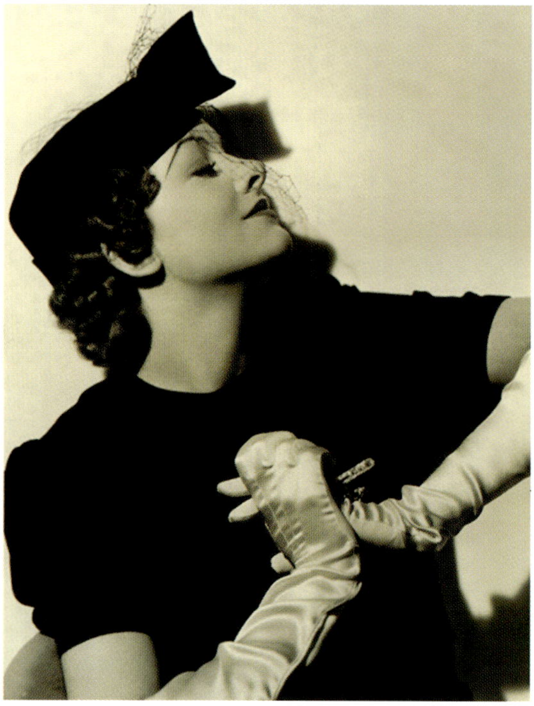

28 Ruth Harriet Louise, *Carmel Myers,* 1925, for *Ben-Hur,* gelatin silver print, 13 x 10 inches

29 Ruth Harriet Louise, *Renée Adorée,* 1926, gelatin silver print, 13 x 10 inches

30 Ruth Harriet Louise, *Dorothy Sebastian,* 1927, for *The Demi-Bride,* gelatin silver print, 13 x 10 inches

31 Ruth Harriet Louise, *Patricia Avery in bunny costume,* 1927, gelatin silver print, 13 x 10 inches

32 Ruth Harriet Louise, *Marion Davies in her garden in Santa Monica,* 1927, gelatin silver print, 13 x 10 inches

33 Ruth Harriet Louise, *Marion Davies,* 1927, gelatin silver print, 13 x 10 inches

34 Ruth Harriet Louise, *Greta Garbo,* 1927, for *Divine Woman,* gelatin silver print, 13 x 10 inches

35 Ruth Harriet Louise, *Mask Photograph* (*Eleanor Boardman*), 1928, gelatin silver print, 13 x 10 inches

36 Ruth Harriet Louise, *Joan Crawford and Robert Montgomery,* 1929, for *Untamed,* gelatin silver print, 13 x 10 inches; *True Romances,* October 1931, painted cover based on photograph

37 Ruth Harriet Louise, *Myrna Loy,* 1936, gelatin silver print, 13 x 10 inches

*Myrna Loy* (above), cat. no. 37
*Joan Crawford and Robert Montgomery* (opposite), cat. no. 36

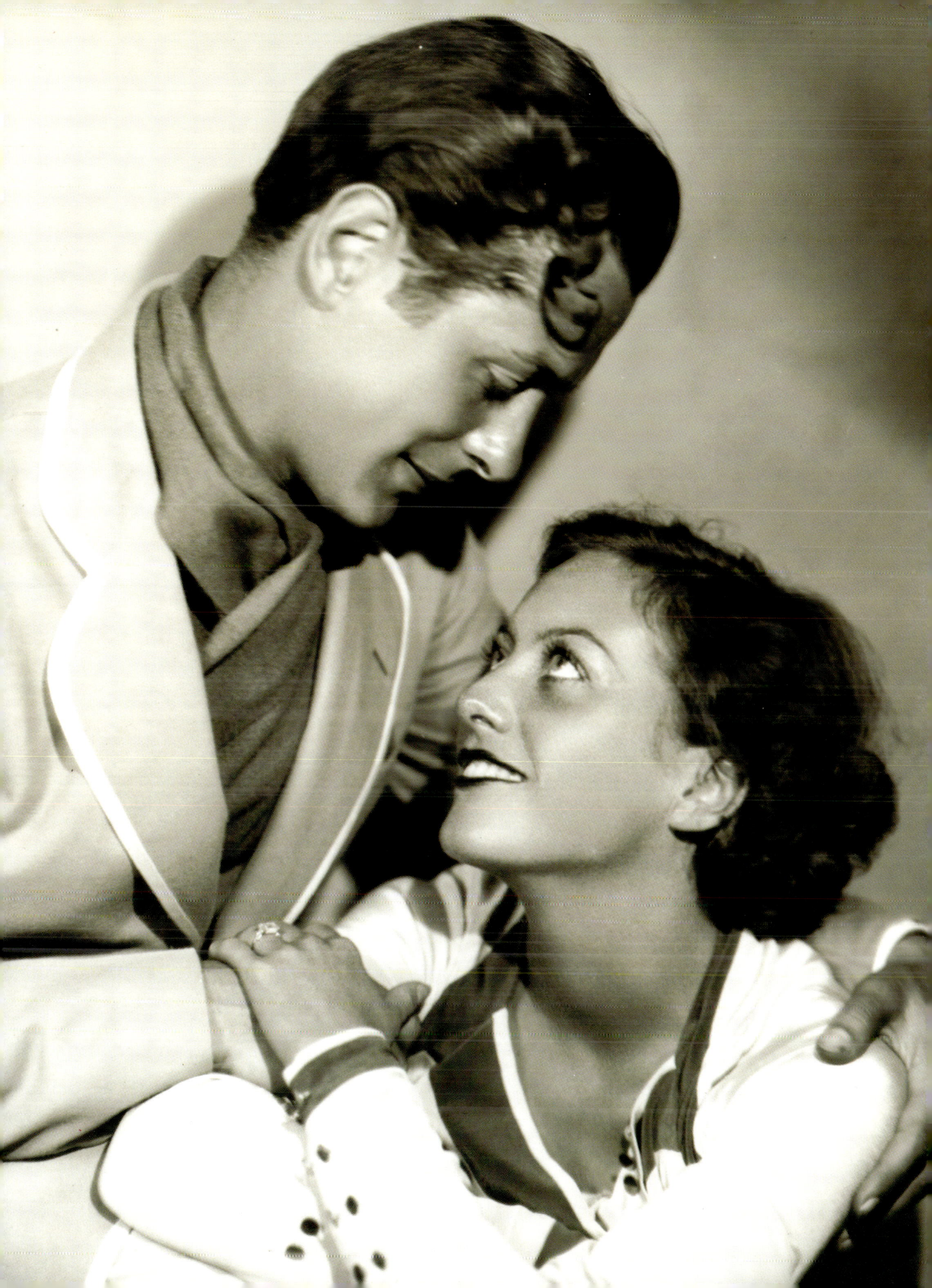

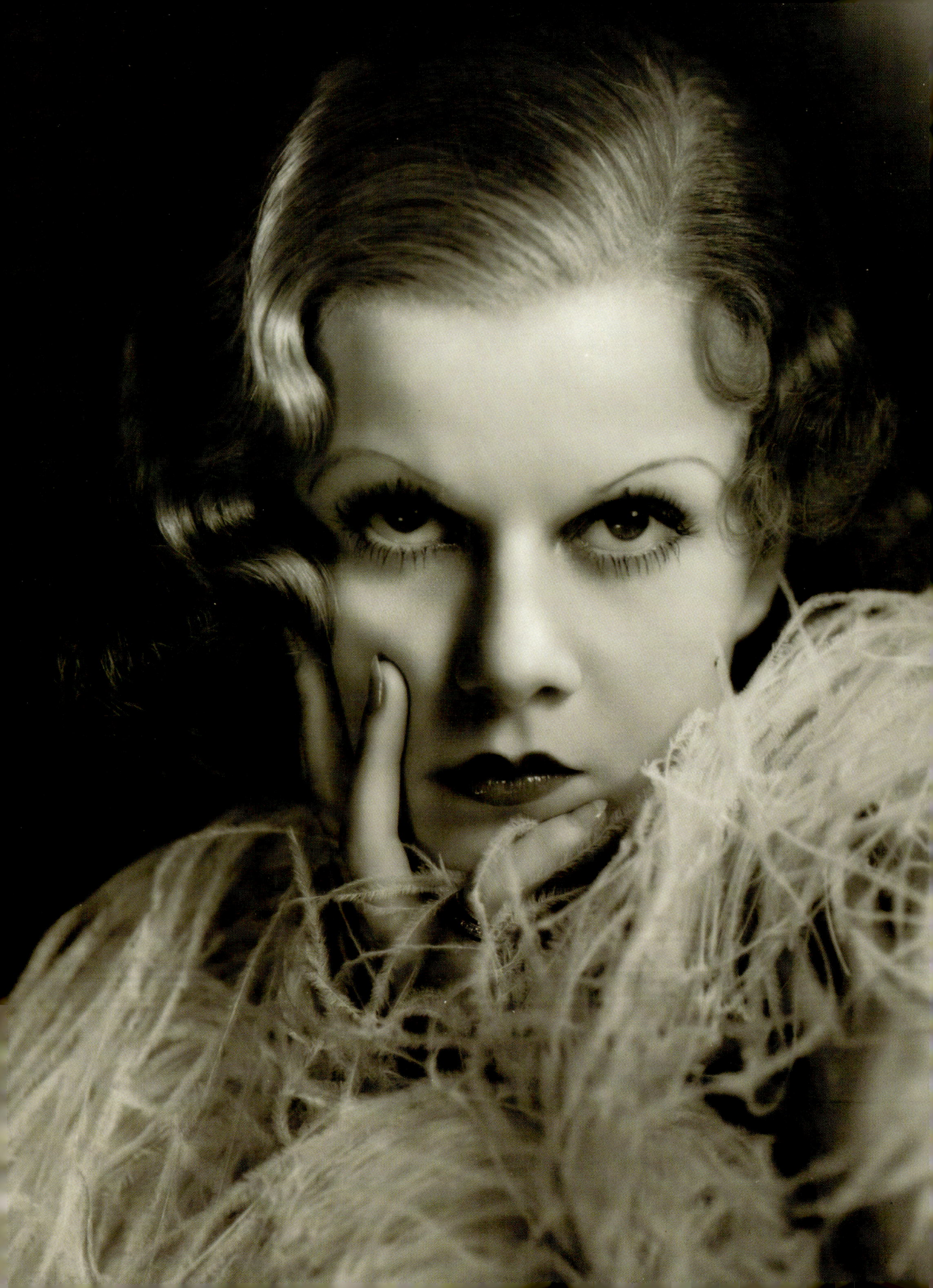

# Clarence Sinclair Bull

Clarence Sinclair Bull (1896–1979) had the longest and most distinguished career of any Hollywood photographer. His first job was with producer Samuel Goldwyn, who hired him in 1919, and when he retired forty-two years later, in 1961, he had photographed nearly every star and featured player who worked in Hollywood, as well as presidents, kings, and other dignitaries visiting his domain at MGM in Culver City. With the organization of MGM in 1924, Bull was appointed head of the large still photography department. He immediately presided over a staff of more than a dozen photographers tasked with documenting MGM's extraordinary output—a new feature film released every week, and hundreds of short subjects every year. In addition, Bull's team took publicity photographs that chronicled the off-screen life of the MGM stock company. In the summer of 1925, when it became evident he needed further assistance, Ruth Harriet Louise was hired as chief portrait photographer. The tense environment this created only ended when Louise left the studio in late 1929.

While Bull never possessed a dramatic eye like George Hurrell, or the superb darkroom technique of his former assistant Eugene Robert Richee, or even the intimacy of Ruth Harriet Louise, this gentlemanly photographer skillfully flattered very different goddesses without resorting to tricky techniques. He varied his lighting and posing with changing photographic styles as Pictorialist blur and Art Deco angularity yielded to modernism's sculptural modeling and extreme close-ups. Backlit blondes like Jean Harlow and Lana Turner glow against inky backgrounds, while the face of brunette Hedy Lamarr is ringed by shadow. With Garbo the artist found his muse. The elegant portraits from their duet over a dozen years, and particularly from 1929–1932, are among the most extraordinary of the millions of star photographs that have been generated by Hollywood.

Bull's career spanned the Golden Age of Hollywood. He was present before the great studios were formed and served until it became clear that a combination of antitrust laws and corporate restructurings would change Hollywood forever. Was it coincidence that 1961, the same year Bull left MGM, saw the American release of Federico Fellini's film *La Dolce Vita* in which a character, Paparazzo, was a tabloid photojournalist who pursued Anita Ekberg? Whether coincidence or not, the early 1960s marked the end of glamour photography and the advent of paparazzi, who opened a new chapter in the presentation of movie stars.

*Jean Harlow*, cat. no. 42

38 Clarence Sinclair Bull, *Lillian Gish,* 1927, for *Annie Laurie,* gelatin silver print, 13⅞ x 10⅞ inches

39 Clarence Sinclair Bull, *Patricia Avery,* 1927, gelatin silver print, 13⅜ x 10⅜ inches

40 Clarence Sinclair Bull, *Greta Garbo,* 1931, for *Mata Hari,* gelatin silver print, 13 x 10⅛ inches

41 Clarence Sinclair Bull, *Leila Hyams,* c. 1932, gelatin silver print, 10 x 13⅛ inches, reproduced in *The New Movie Magazine,* February 1931

42 Clarence Sinclair Bull, *Jean Harlow,* 1932, for *Red-Headed Woman,* gelatin silver print, 13 x 10 inches

43 Clarence Sinclair Bull, *Jean Harlow and Clark Gable,* 1936, for *Saratoga,* gelatin silver print, 13 x 10⅛ inches

44 Clarence Sinclair Bull, *Clark Gable and Lana Turner,* 1940, for *Honky Tonk,* gelatin silver print, 10½ x 13½ inches

45 Clarence Sinclair Bull, *Hedy Lamarr,* c. 1942, gelatin silver print, 13 x 10 inches

*Leila Hyams,* cat. no. 41

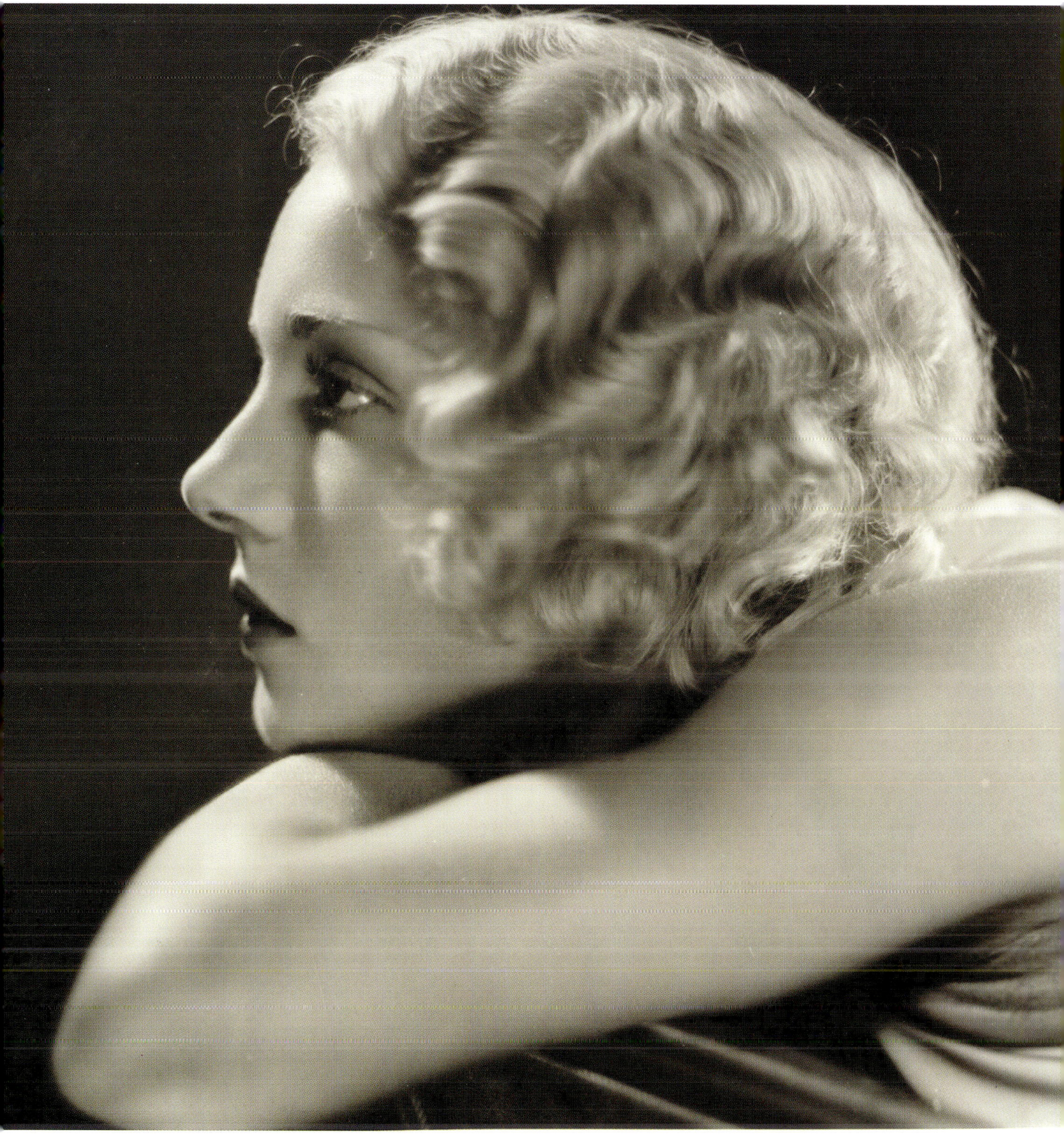

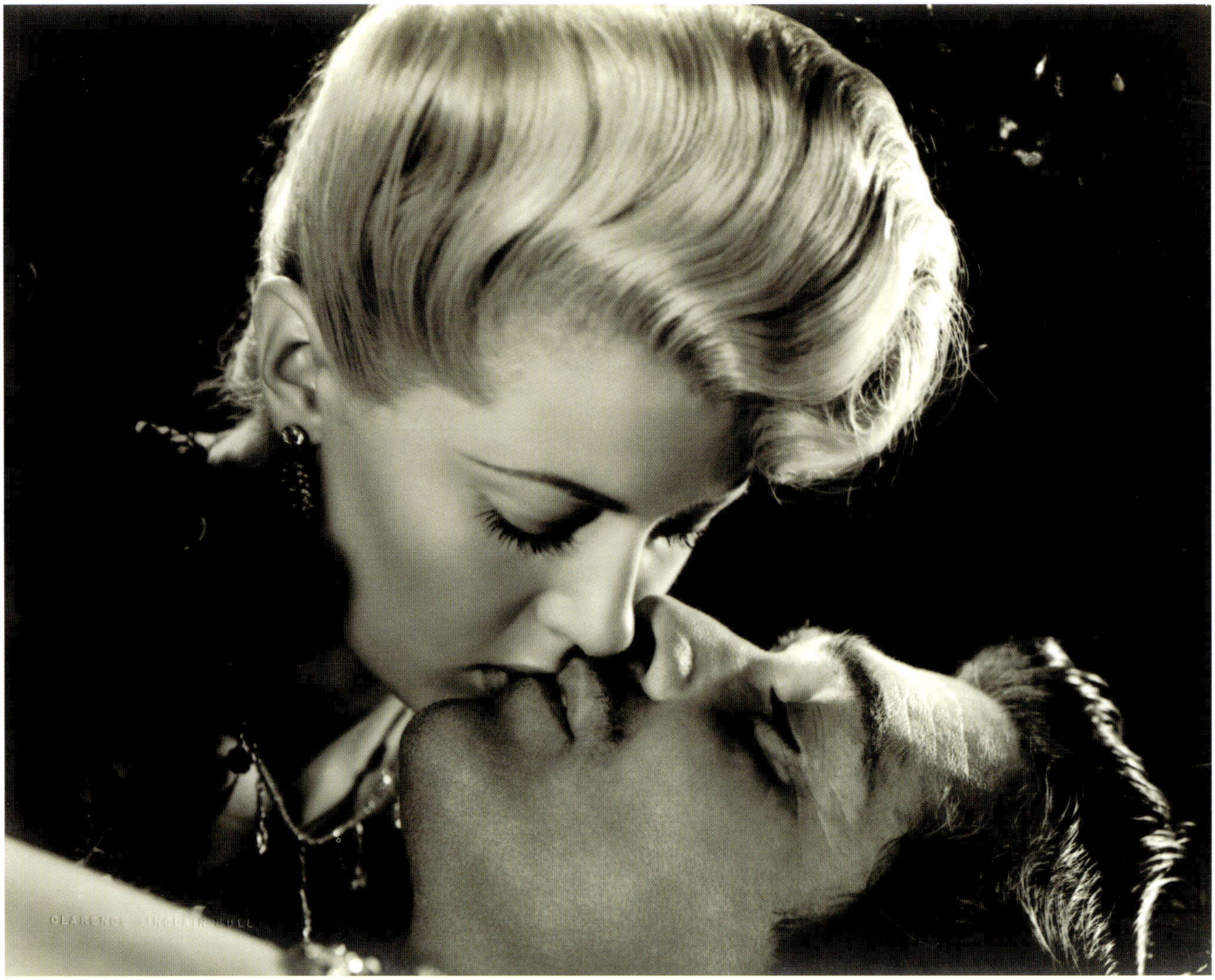

*Clark Gable and Lana Turner* (above), cat. no. 44
*Hedy Lamarr* (opposite), cat. no. 45

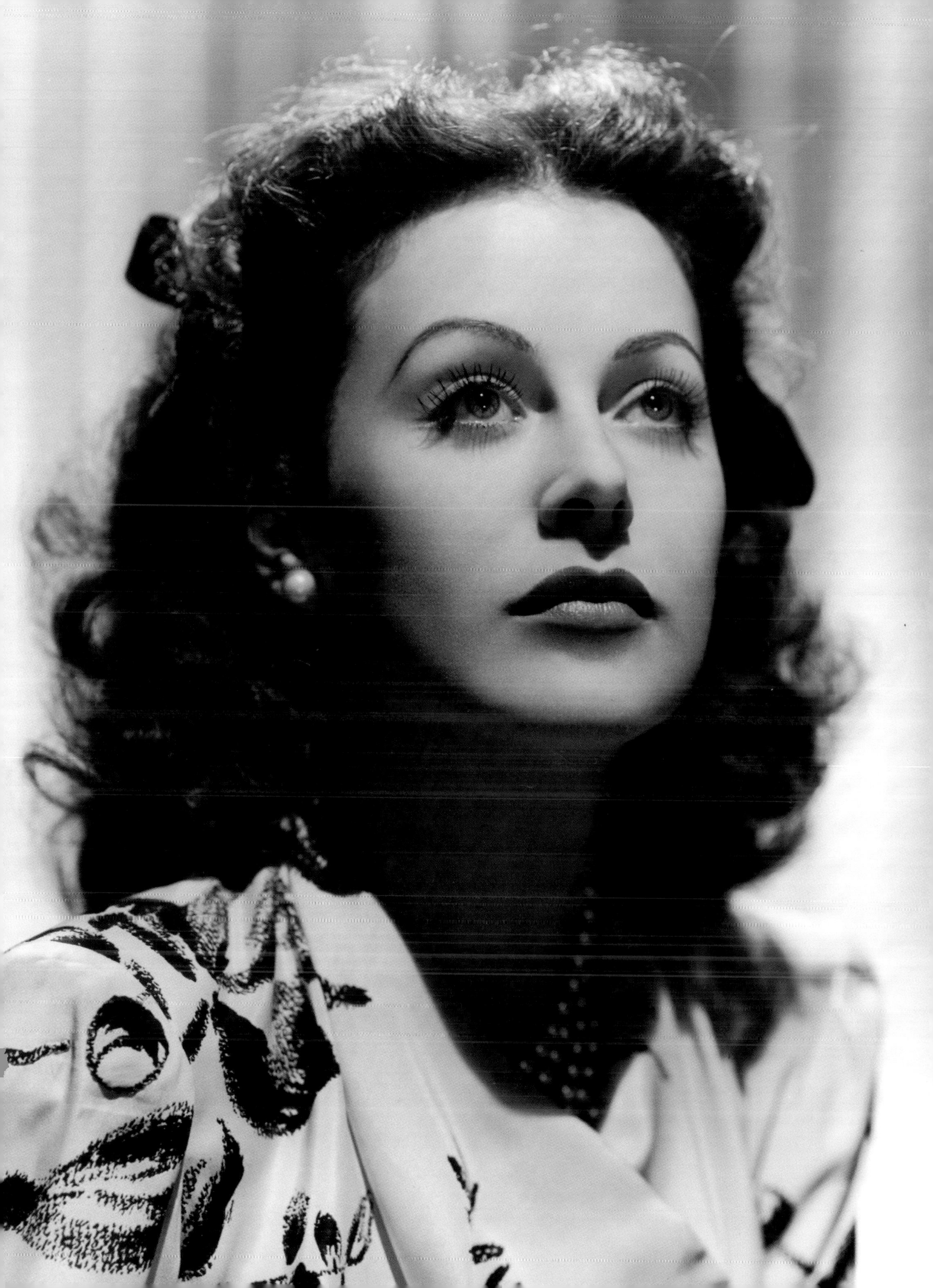

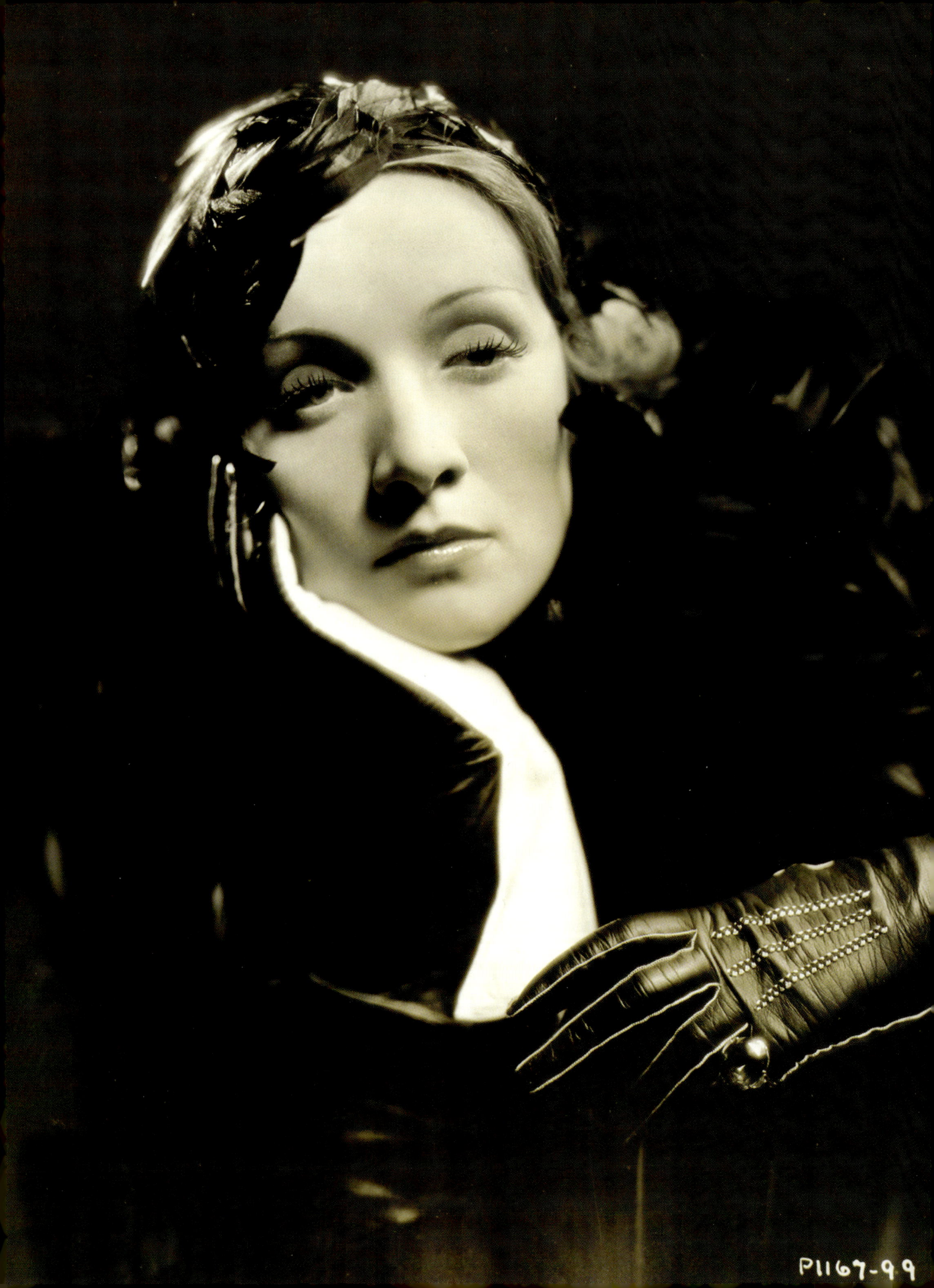
P1167-99

# Paramount Photographers

The company that became the mighty Paramount Pictures began in the earliest days of motion pictures. In 1912 Adolph Zukor launched the Famous Players Film Company, and through a series of strategic mergers Paramount Pictures was born in 1925. Zukor was among the first studio executives to decide to bring all aspects of film production under the direct supervision of the studios. This included the portrait and still departments, ending most free-lance arrangements.

Eugene Robert Richee (1896–1972) ran Paramount's portrait gallery from 1925 to 1941 and was responsible for the sleek, glamorous image of its actresses, especially in the silent days when Clara Bow, Louise Brooks, and Bebe Daniels were top draws, and in the early talkie era when Marlene Dietrich rivaled Greta Garbo as Hollywood's supreme love goddess. Richee was a master of composition and lighting, producing some of the most technically beautiful prints of any studio portraitist.

Assisting Richee was Otto Dyar (1892–1988) who started as a stills photographer on set and assumed portrait work in the late 1920s. Although he got his start photographing Clara Bow in candids taken outside the studio, his subjects were primarily second-tier actresses such as Ziegfeld star Lillian Roth (portrayed in 1929, the year she signed her Paramount contract) and comedienne Thelma Todd.

William Walling came to Paramount in the early 1930s, beginning his career as a stills photographer. He established his reputation with Josef von Sternberg productions starring Dietrich such as *Shanghai Express* and *Blond Venus* (both released in 1932). His talent recognized, he took over a portrait studio when Dyar left Paramount in 1933.

Still and portrait photography was, for some, a first step toward a career with the motion picture camera. Elwood Bredell (1884–1976) was originally an actor, but by the early 1930s he was hired by Paramount as a still photographer who occasionally made portraits. In 1937 he began a distinguished career as a cinematographer working primarily at Universal.

Paramount competed with MGM during the 1930s as the most prestigious film company, by establishing the glamorous personas of comediennes such as Mae West and Carole Lombard and actresses Claudette Colbert and Dorothy Lamour. Richee photographed them all and played an important role in the creation of their images. He left Paramount in 1941 as the great glamour era was fading.

*Marlene Dietrich,* cat. no. 49

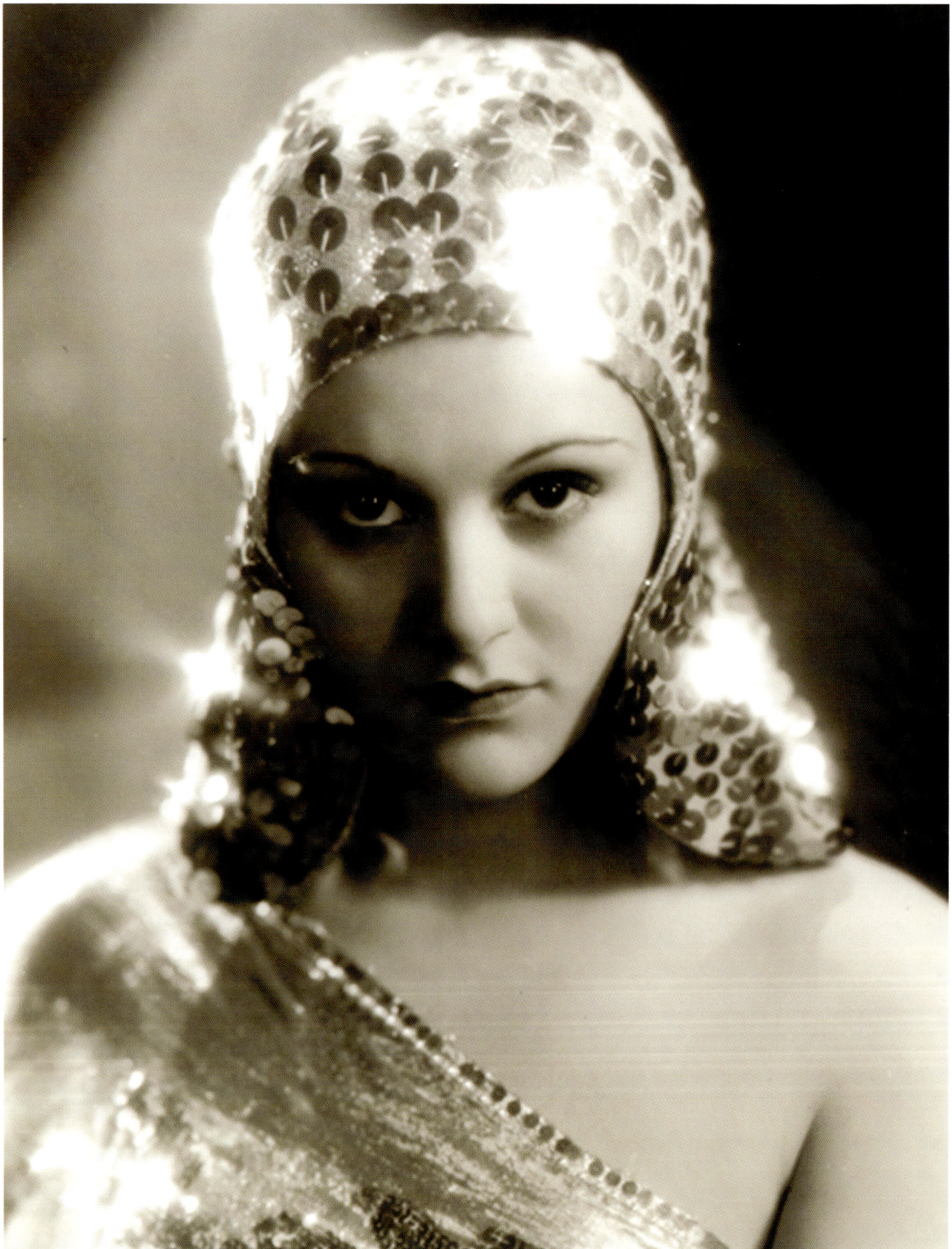

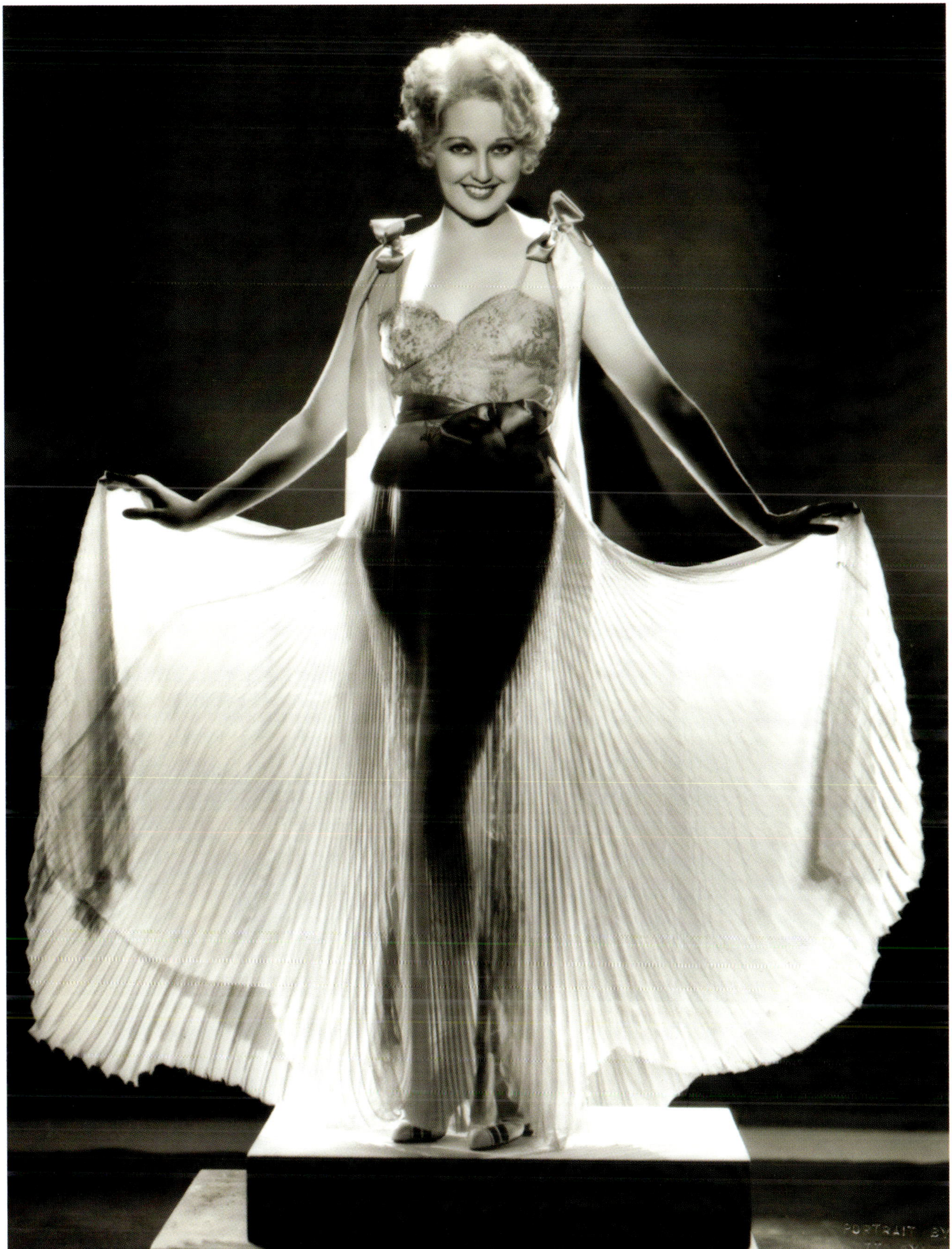
PORTRAIT BY

46 Eugene Robert Richee, *Bebe Daniels,* 1927, for *She's a Sheik,* gelatin silver print, 14 x 11 inches

47 Eugene Robert Richee, *Clara Bow,* 1928, gelatin silver print, 13 x 10 inches

48 Otto Dyar, *Lillian Roth,* 1929, for *The Love Parade,* gelatin silver print, 13 x 10

49 Eugene Robert Richee, *Marlene Dietrich,* 1932, for *Shanghai Express,* gelatin silver print, 10 x 8 inches

50 Otto Dyar, *Thelma Todd,* 1932, for *This is the Night,* gelatin silver print, 13 x 10

51 William Walling, *Marlene Dietrich,* 1934, for *The Devil is a Woman,* gelatin silver print, 14 x 11 inches; printed c. 1995 from an original 8 x 10-inch negative

52 Elwood Bredell, *Anna May Wong,* 1934, for *Limehouse Blues,* gelatin silver print, 13 x 10 inches; reproduced in *Photoplay,* December 1934 (reversed)

53 William Walling, *Dorothy Lamour,* 1941, for *Man About Town,* gelatin silver print, 13 x 10 inches

*Lillian Roth* (page 50), cat. no. 48
*Thelma Todd* (page 51), cat. no. 50
*Clara Bow* (opposite) cat. no. 47

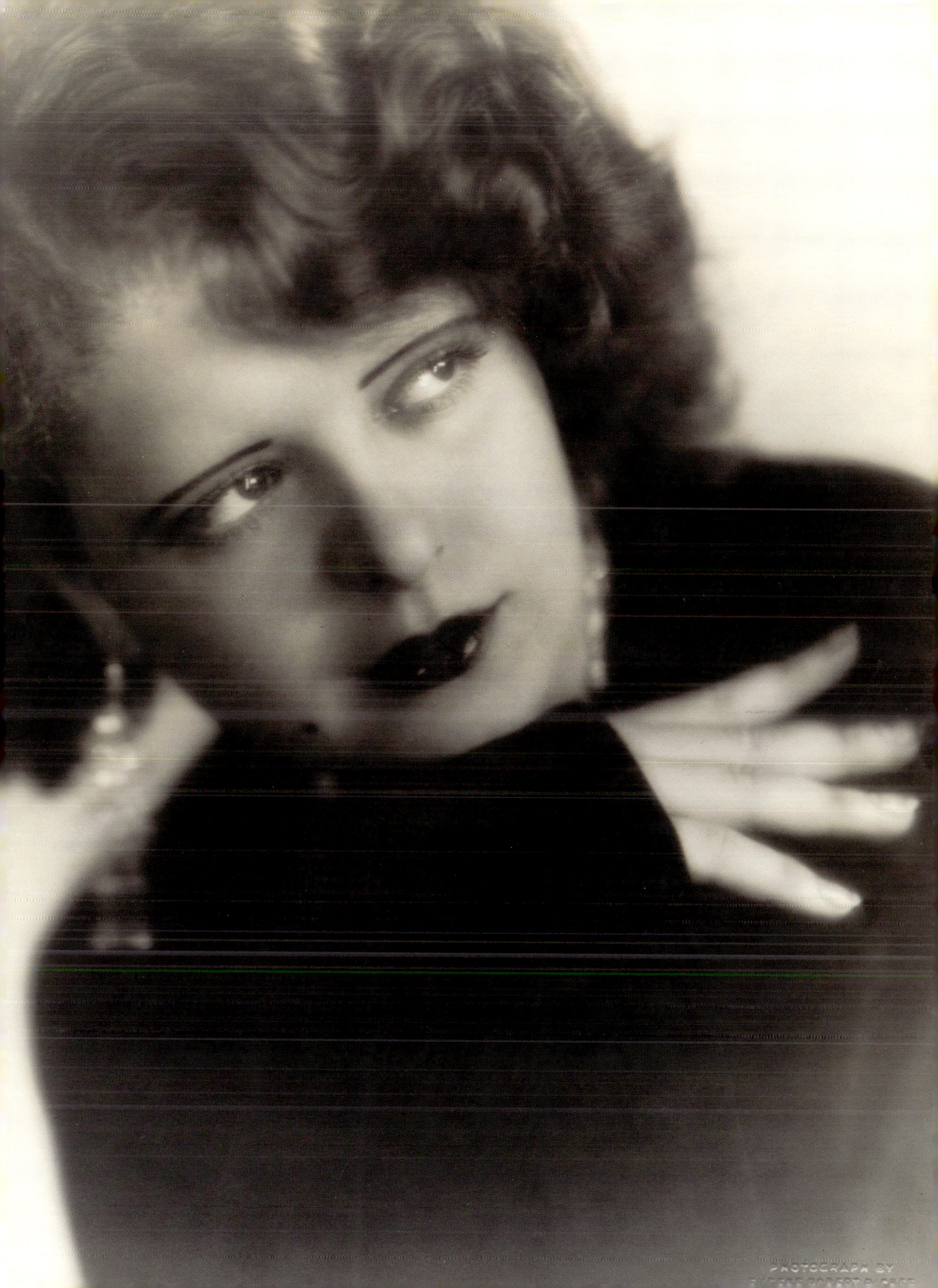
PHOTOGRAPH BY

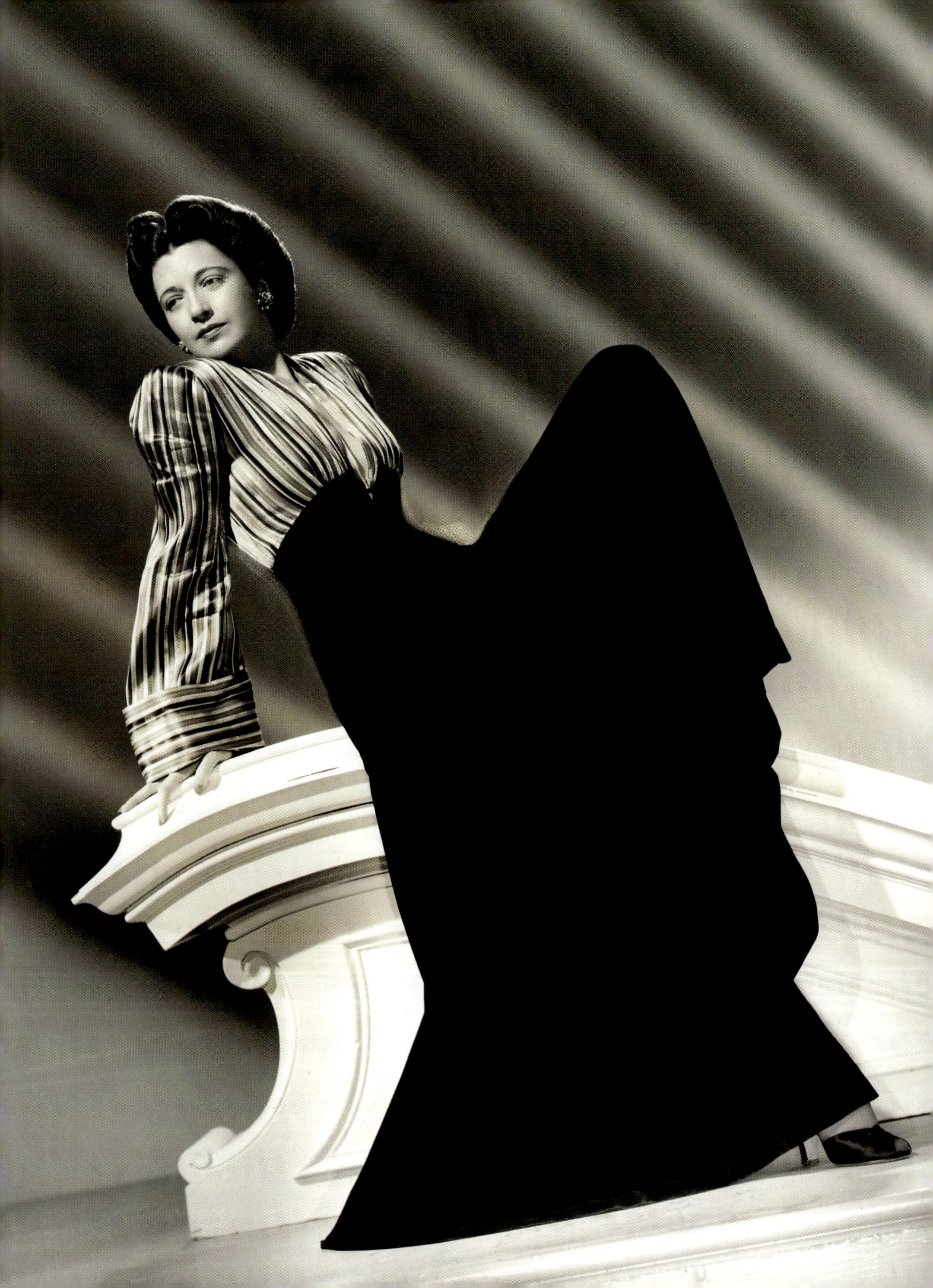

# Stars in Fashion

In the 1920s and 1930s female stars dominated Hollywood filmmaking. There were plenty of men who deserved becoming legends—Gary Cooper, Clark Gable, Cary Grant—but for the most part it was the actresses who brought audiences into the theaters. Glamorous figures like Gloria Swanson and Greta Garbo became feminine role models in the silent era. When Joan Crawford appeared on the screen with a new hairstyle, she was imitated by millions of women. If industry reports are accurate, a white ruffled dress she wore in *Letty Lynton* (1932) sold 500,000 copies.

The studios made little income from these sales, but they did know that beautifully dressed stars—whether seen in films or in print—kept female audiences buying movie tickets, particularly in the Depression years. At the biggest, best capitalized studios like MGM and Paramount, costumes were as important as sets, and as much attention was paid to dress as locations. Stylish actresses with exquisite makeup, hairstyles, and clothing let women around the world enter a perfect fantasy.

From the early 1930s studio portrait photographers focused on the costumes and "personal" dress of leading ladies. Newspapers and fan magazines wanted to publish not only the latest portrait of an attractive star but also her latest outfits. Top dress designers such as Gilbert Adrian at MGM and Travis Bainton at Paramount turned out thousands of styles each year, from period costumes to the smartest contemporary fashions. Actresses were bound by contract to appear in public as modishly garbed as they appeared on the screen. So studio designers provided day and evening wear that mirrored the sorts of dress their characters would portray in their films. Even a publicity-averse actress like Garbo became a fashion icon: despite her refusal to make public appearances, her slacks, sunglasses, and slouch hats became famous and widely copied. Crawford, on the other hand, never missed an opportunity to show off a new dress. Some actresses, such as Carmel Myers and most importantly Kay Francis, were as famous for their fashion sense as they were for their acting.

High-end fashion and celebrity journals like *Vogue* and *Vanity Fair* were as eager as fan magazines to illustrate the stars in costume, their "own" dress, or the editors' selections of couture. The stars alternated with socialites and models for Edward Steichen, Cecil Beaton, Nickolas Muray and similar chic photographers. Meanwhile, Hollywood's studio portraitists supplied elegant new photographs free and frequently to these media.

*Kay Francis,* cat. no. 63

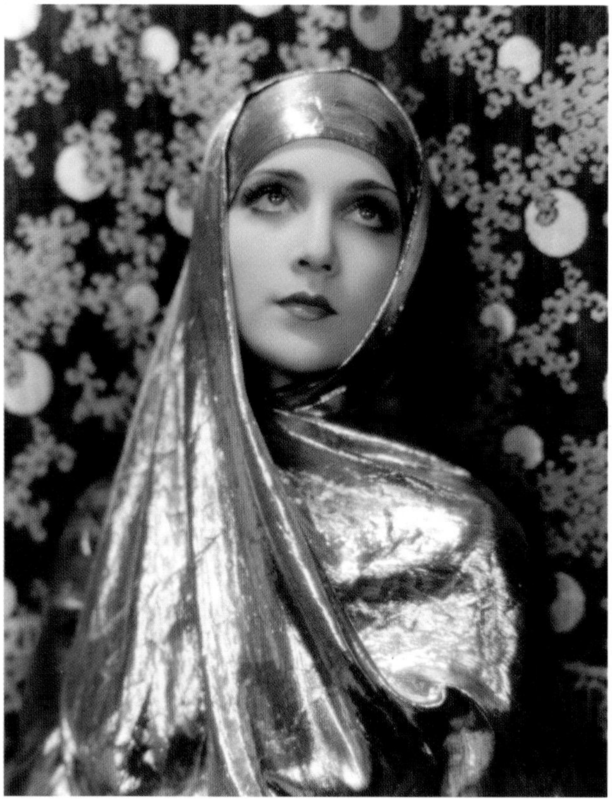

54 Ruth Harriet Louise, *Marion Davies,* c. 1927, gelatin silver print, 13 x 10 inches

55 Ruth Harriet Louise, *Joan Crawford,* 1928, gelatin silver print, 13 x 10 inches, reproduced in *Photoplay,* October 1929

56 William E. Thomas, *Carole Lombard,* 1928, gelatin silver print, 10 x 8 inches

57 Clarence Bull, *Madge Evans,* c. 1930, gelatin silver print, 14 x 11 inches

58 Elmer Fryer, *Carmel Myers,* 1931, gelatin silver print, 14 x 11 inches

59 Clarence Sinclair Bull, *Joan Crawford,* c. 1931, gelatin silver print, 13 x 10 inches, inscribed in Crawford's hand: *Betty*

60 Clarence Sinclair Bull, *Greta Garbo,* 1931, for *Inspiration,* gelatin silver print, 13 x 10 inches

61 Ernest A. Bachrach, *Irene Dunne,* c. 1934, gelatin silver print, 14 x 11 inches

62 Clarence Sinclair Bull, *Norma Shearer and Louella Parsons,* c. 1935, gelatin silver print, 10 x 13 inches

63 Ray Jones, *Kay Francis,* 1941, gelatin silver print, 10 x 8 inches

*Carole Lombard* (above), cat. no. 56
*Irene Dunne* (opposite), cat. no. 61

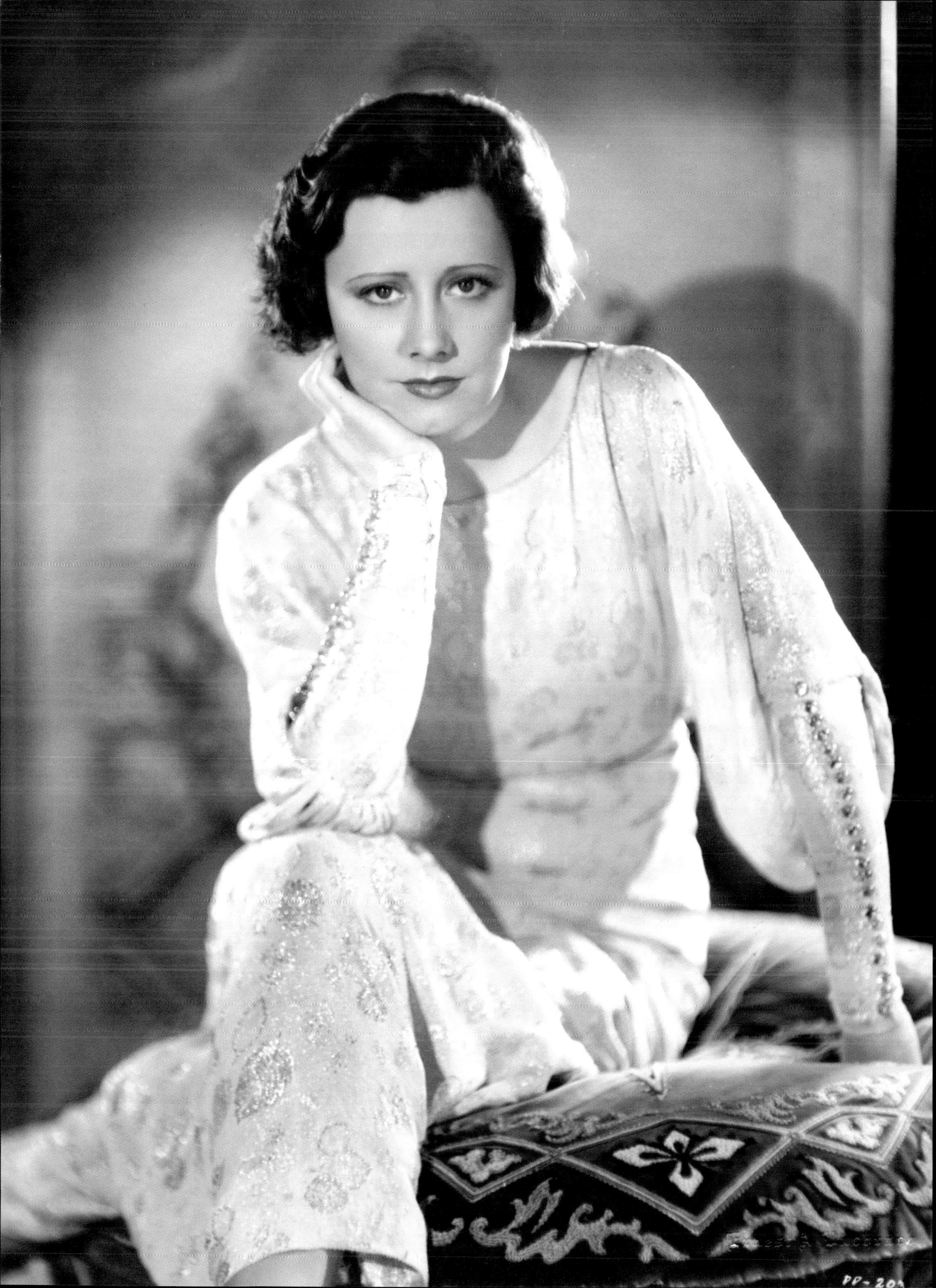

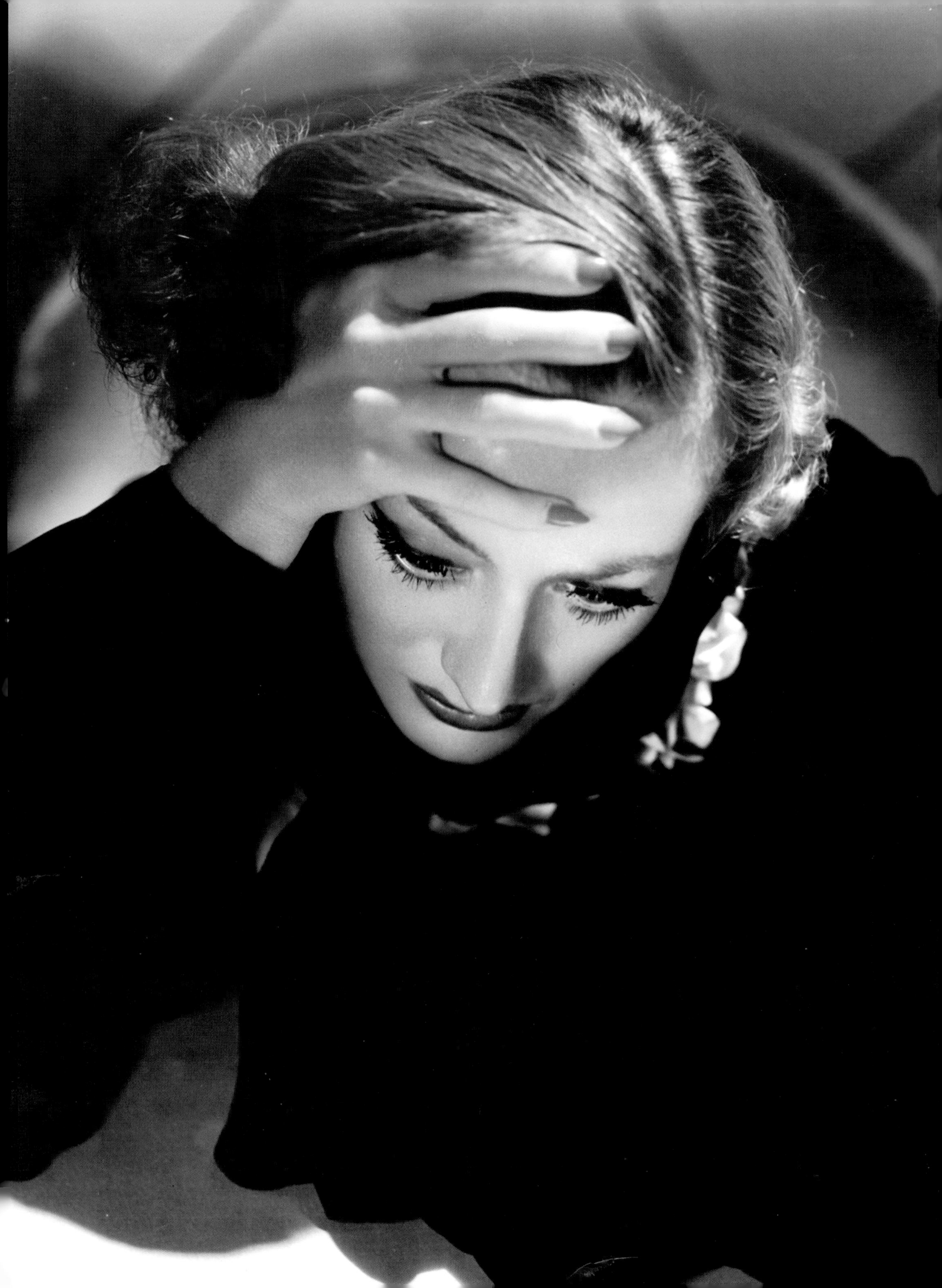

# Joan Crawford

When Joan Crawford (1905–1977) signed a six-month contract with MGM in December 1924, she was one among hundreds of attractive, untested young women who traveled to California with dreams of movie stardom. Just eighteen and dancing at a West 56th nightclub in New York, she was offered her chance after one of MGM's top producers saw her in a chorus line of dancers. Born Lucille LeSueur and working under the name Billie Cassin, she would take a new name—invented in Hollywood—and become one of Hollywood's biggest stars.

Crawford began her Hollywood career slowly, in small parts, and finally graduated to featured roles. In 1927, she appeared in seven pictures with some of the most popular male actors, John Gilbert, William Haines, and Lon Chaney. As the lead in *Our Dancing Daughters* (1928) Crawford showed she had the qualities of a headliner. Upon her marriage in 1929 to Hollywood "royalty" Douglas Fairbanks, Jr., MGM anointed her its newest star.

Ruthlessly ambitious, Crawford strategically plotted her climb to the top. This included posing for any and all publicity pictures. She was among the first actresses to model clothing for department stores, always under the watchful eye of MGM's publicity department. Collaborating with Ruth Harriet Louise in the portrait studio, she was transformed from a pretty but uninspiring face into a vibrant avatar of the New Woman.

Although Crawford was a star in the last days of silent pictures, her reputation derives from her work in the 1930s and 1940s. In film after film she portrayed the shop girl or young woman from the wrong side of the tracks who prevails though determination, always getting her man—usually Clark Gable. To promote these movies she worked closely with Louise, Clarence Sinclair Bull, and with most synergy, George Hurrell.

Looking back over all the stars of twentieth-century films, it may be that Crawford had the greatest career of all. She was a star in silent pictures and an icon in the 1930s. Fired by Louis B. Mayer in 1943, she was signed by Warner Brothers where she became an electrifying dramatic actress, garnering multiple Academy Award nominations and the statue for *Mildred Pierce* (1945). Success continued through the 1950s, and in 1962 she was mesmerizing in *Whatever Happened to Baby Jane*. At her death in 1977, director George Cukor, with whom she worked many times, described Crawford as "the perfect image of a movie star."

*Joan Crawford,* cat. no. 73

64 Ruth Harriet Louise, *Joan Crawford,* gelatin silver print, 1926, 13 x 10 inches

65 Ruth Harriet Louise, *Joan Crawford,* gelatin silver print, 1926, 13 x 10 inches

66 Ruth Harriet Louise, *Joan Crawford in Santa's helper costume,* gelatin silver print, 1927, 13 x 10 inches

67 Ruth Harriet Louise, *Joan Crawford,* gelatin silver print, 1928, 13 x 10 inches

68 Ruth Harriet Louise, *Joan Crawford with tennis racket,* gelatin silver print, 1929, 10 x 13 inches

69 Clarence Sinclair Bull, *Joan Crawford,* gelatin silver print, 1931, 13 x 10 inches

70 Clarence Sinclair Bull, *Joan Crawford as a blonde,* gelatin silver print, 1931, 13 x 10 inches; reproduced in *Silver Screen*, June 1931

71 George Hurrell, *Joan Crawford,* gelatin silver print, c. 1932, 13 x 10 inches

72 George Hurrell, *Joan Crawford,* 1933, for *Dancing Lady,* gelatin silver print, 10 x 13 inches

73 George Hurrell, *Joan Crawford,* 1933, for *Dancing Lady,* gelatin silver print, 12 x 9 inches

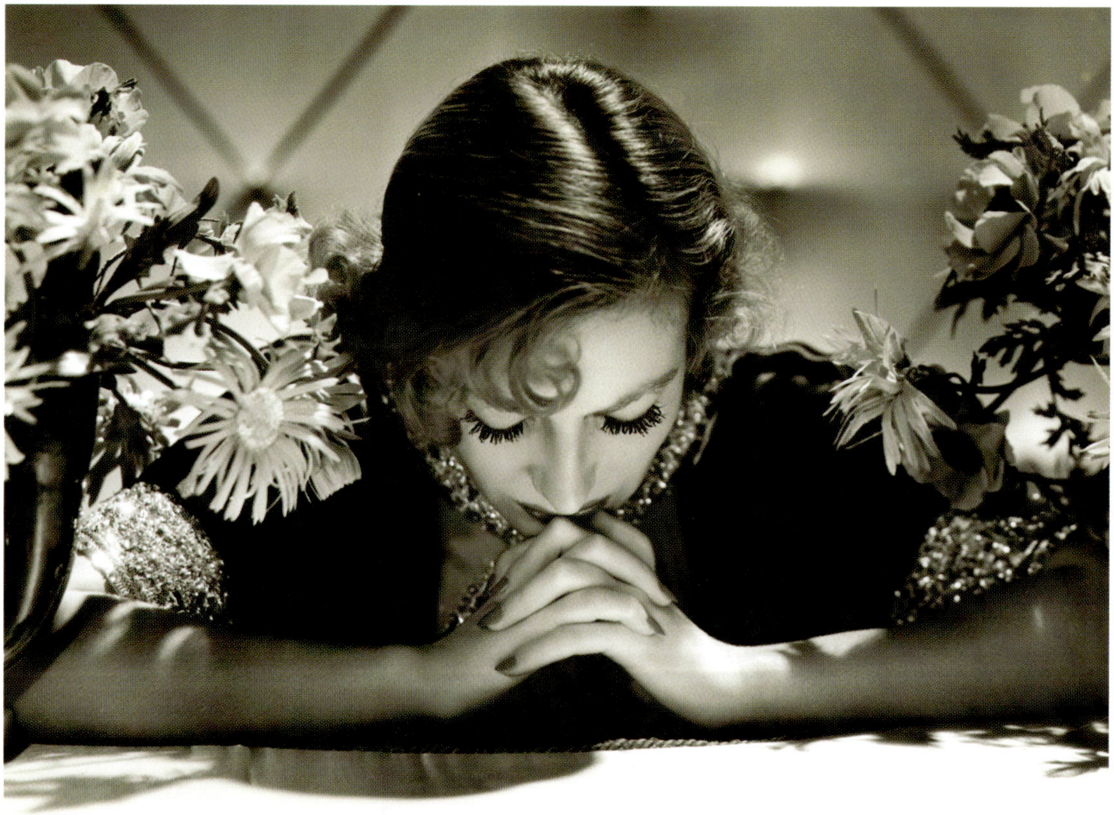

*Joan Crawford* (above), cat. no. 72
*Joan Crawford* (opposite), cat. no. 64

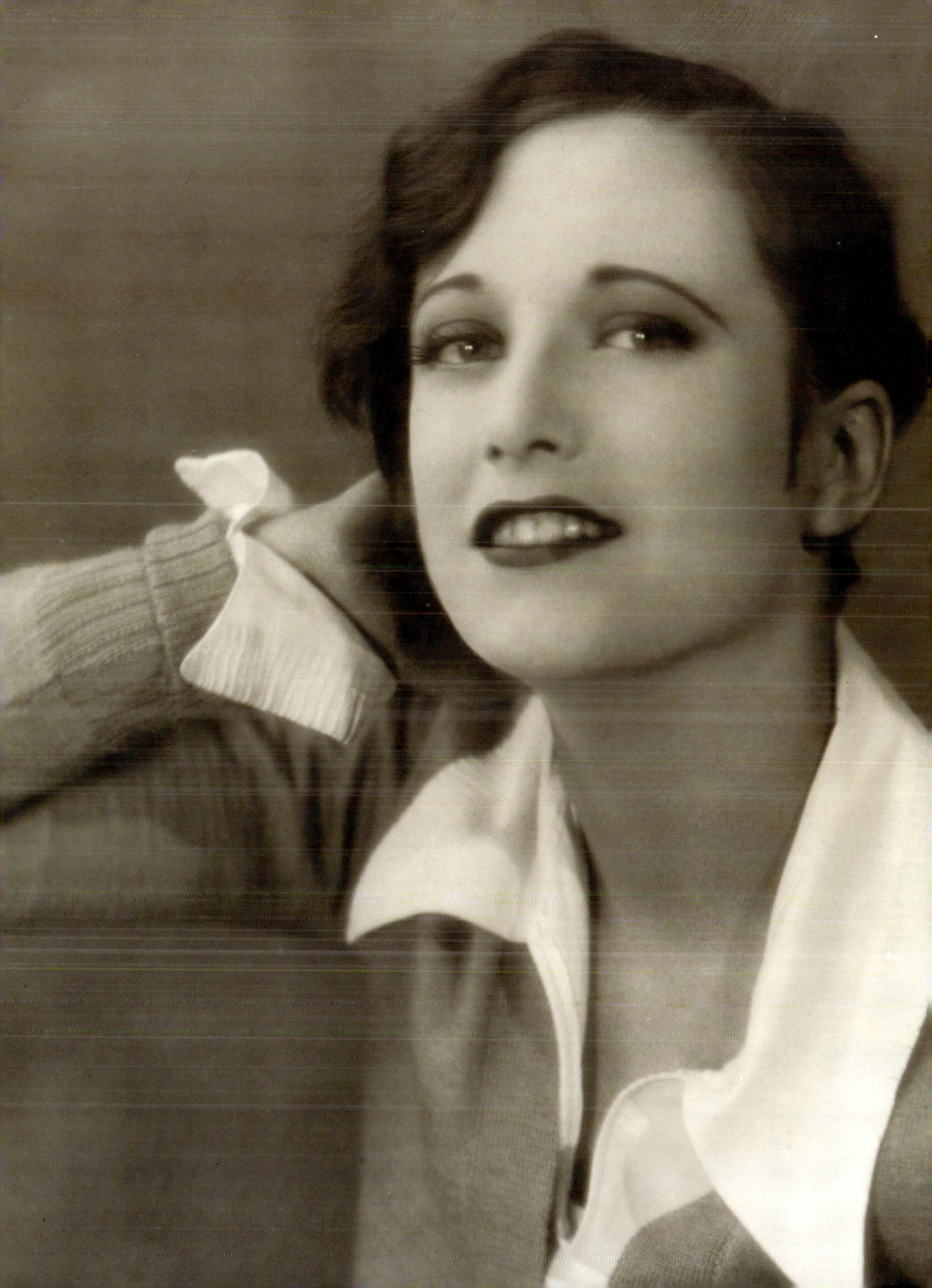

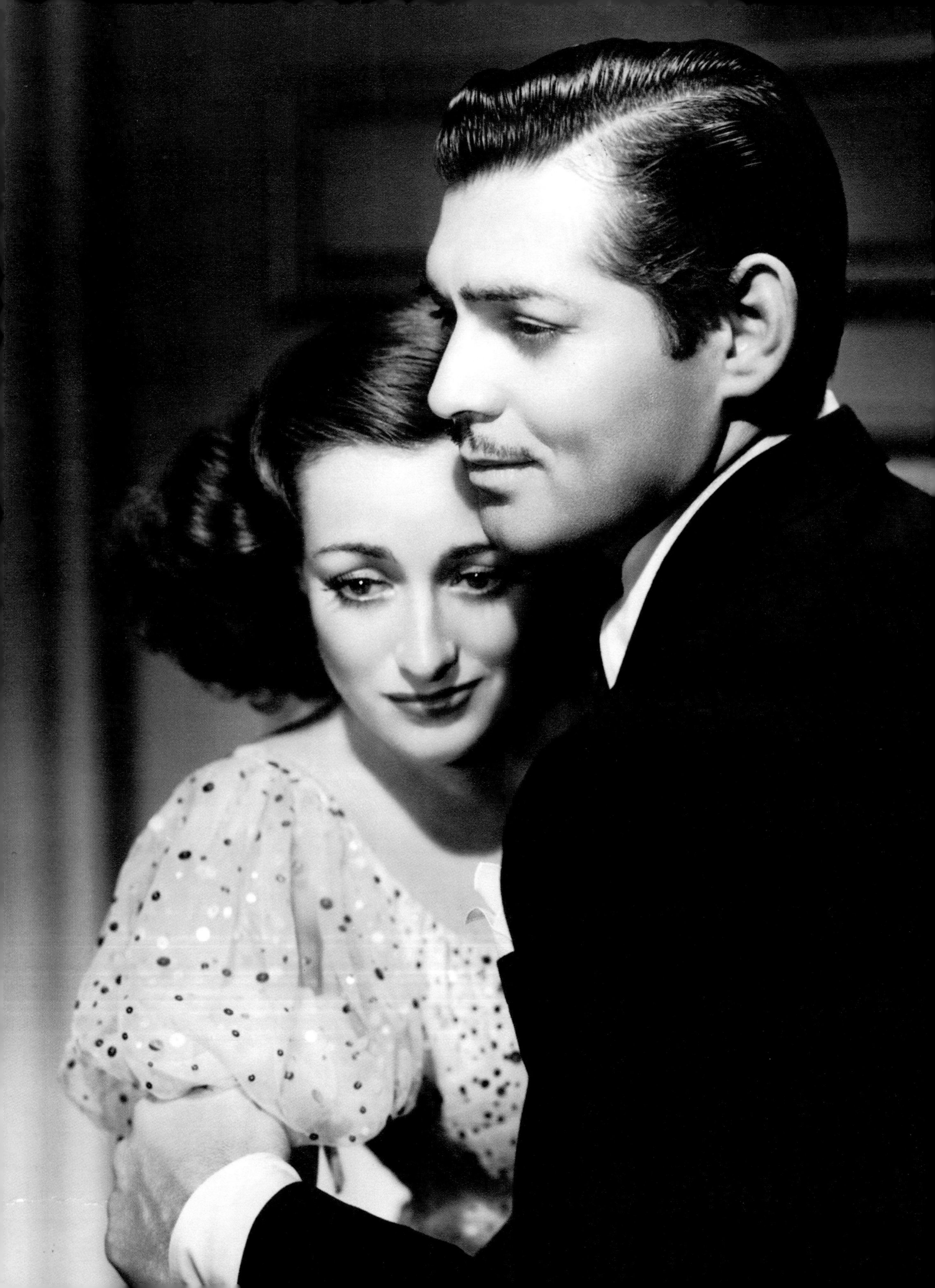

# George Hurrell

The portraits of George Hurrell (1904–1992), particularly from the 1930s, brought Hollywood photography to its pinnacle. Working privately out of a studio in Laguna Beach, California, in 1930 Hurrell was hired by MGM to replace Ruth Harriet Louise. He would create the iconic images of Joan Crawford, Jean Harlow, and Jane Russell, among other stars, and influence the look of star portraits for more than two decades.

First Ramon Novarro and later Norma Shearer (who was married to MGM chief of production Irving Thalberg) had gone off the studio lot to take advantage of Hurrell's innovative style of portraiture when he was still independent. Shearer was an attractive actress with an elegant profile and a substantial career in silent pictures. She felt deeply competitive, however, with Joan Crawford and especially Garbo, and believed Louise served her rivals better in assisting them through portraits to land coveted sensual romantic roles. She sought a photographer who might reveal her dramatic fire. With George Hurrell she found the right man.

Hurrell introduced razor-sharp focus to studio photography and created lighting that gave bold patterns of dark and light: his subjects project from his prints with the effervescence and graphic beauty now synonymous with Hollywood imagery and modernist design. Under Hurrell's megawatt lamps and heavy retouching, Shearer became the goddess she so longed to portray. Hurrell's portraits helped her win her first risqué role, *The Divorcée* (1930), and she won an Oscar for this film in her new guise. In subsequent portraits she sizzles, obviously enjoying the rapport of their sittings.

But it was Crawford who became the quintessential Hurrell subject. He recognized her total determination to become a reigning star, and the two joined forces to show Crawford off—with her large-featured face mirroring changing emotions, with various props, and with a profligate array of costumes and stylish clothes. Hurrell also served Jean Harlow brilliantly. The platinum blonde, who came to MGM in 1931, might never have become the screen's sex goddess of the 1930s without his blazing lights and control of her uninhibited physicality.

Hurrell was part of the artistic vanguard and as such his talents were quickly seized upon not only by MGM, where he remained for only four years, but by other stars and studios who could afford his extravagant fees. After the war, he relocated to New York where he worked for magazines, and only late in his career did he return to Hollywood and the glamour of which he is the undisputed master.

*Joan Crawford and Clark Gable,* cat. no. 82

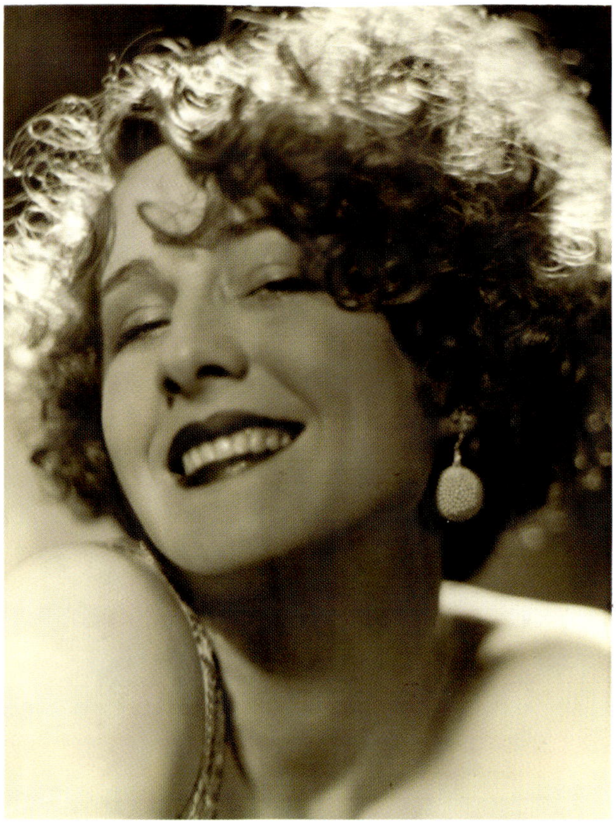

74 George Hurrell, *Norma Shearer,* 1930, gelatin silver print, 13 x 10 inches

75 George Hurrell, *Norma Shearer,* 1932, for *Smilin' Through,* gelatin silver print, 13 x 10 inches

76 George Hurrell, *Joan Crawford, Lionel Barrymore, and John Barrymore,* 1932, for *Grand Hotel,* gelatin silver print, 10 x 13 inches

77 George Hurrell, *Joan Crawford and Franchot Tone,* 1933, for *Dancing Lady,* gelatin silver print, 13 x 10 inches

78 George Hurrell, *Adrianne Ames,* 1934, gelatin silver print, 14 x 11 inches

79 George Hurrell, *Jean Harlow,* c. 1934, gelatin silver print, 10 x 8 inches

80 George Hurrell, *Jean Harlow,* c. 1934, gelatin silver print, 10 x 8 inches

81 George Hurrell, *Ann Sothern,* 1936, for *Save a Lady,* gelatin silver print, 14 x 11 inches

82 George Hurrell, *Joan Crawford and Clark Gable,* 1936, for *Love on the Run,* gelatin silver print, 13 x 10 inches

83 George Hurrell, *Ann Sheridan,* 1939, gelatin silver print, 14 x 11 inches, printed c. 1995 from an original 8 x 10-inch negative

*Norma Shearer* (above), cat. no. 74
*Ann Sothern* (opposite), cat. no. 82

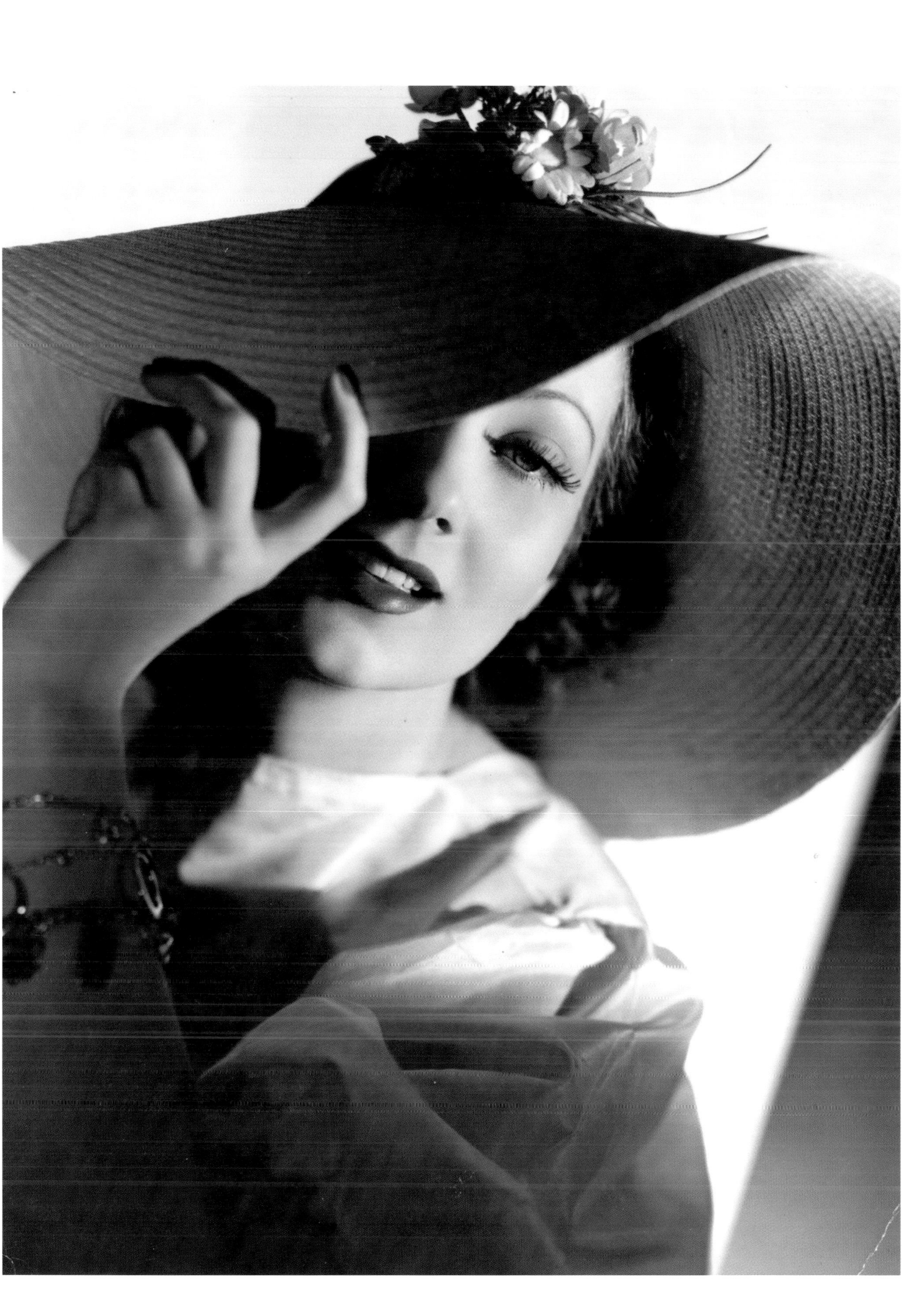

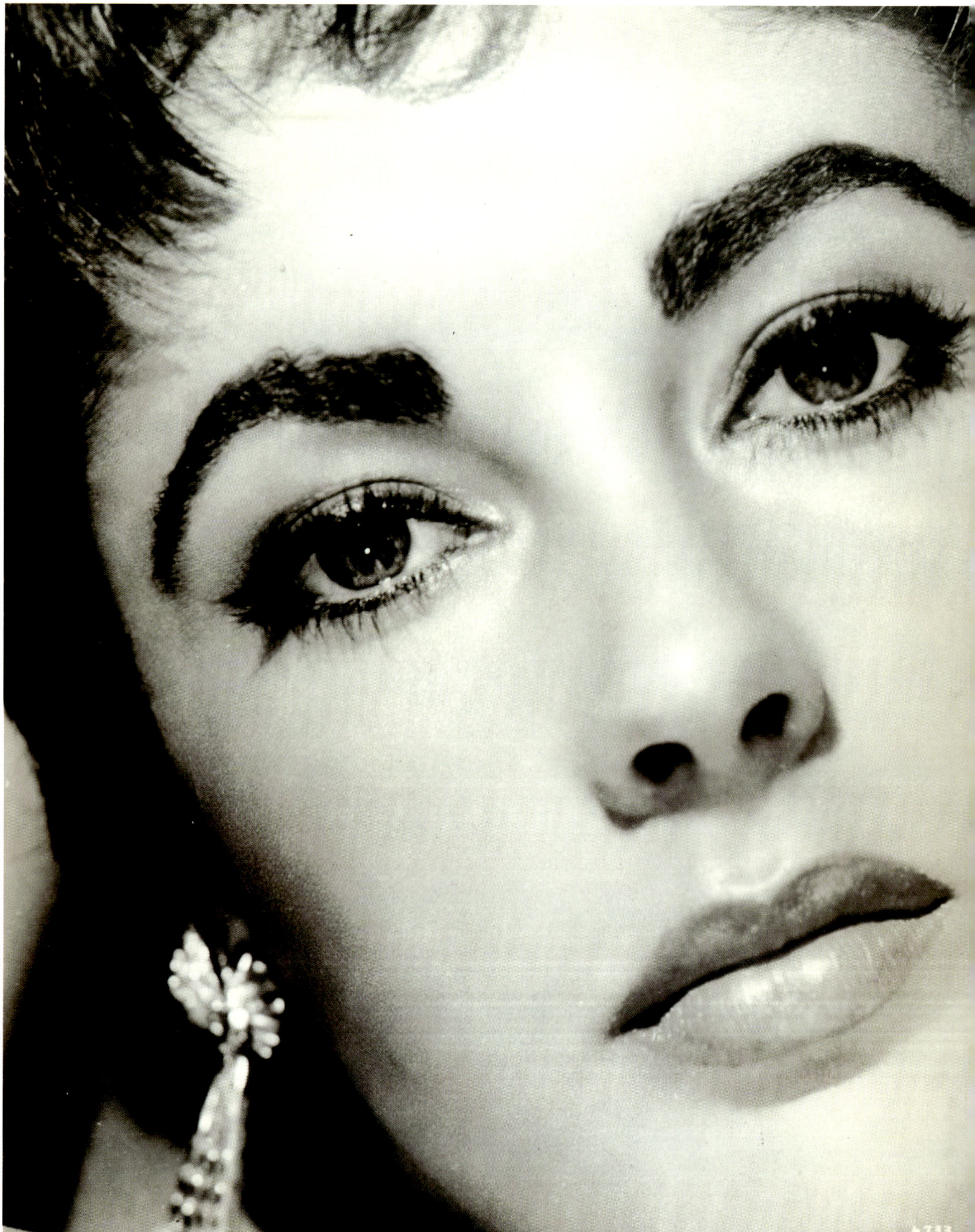
6733

# Elizabeth Taylor

Elizabeth Taylor (1932–2011) was the last great star produced by the Hollywood studio system. She started out as a delightful child actress, scoring in *National Velvet* (1944) when she was twelve. By the early 1950s she began to assume adult roles, and in one of her first, as the lead in *A Place in the Sun* (1951), she displayed an exquisite beauty and subtlety of acting that augured a brilliant career. She was impeccably managed by MGM throughout the 1950s and scored triumphs in *Giant* (1956) and *Cat on a Hot Tin Roof* (1958). In 1961, finally free of her MGM contract, she signed to star in *Cleopatra* for the unprecedented salary of one million dollars. At that moment she seemed to be at the height of her beauty, talent, and fame—the perfect definition of what Andy Warhol termed a superstar. But it was only the climax of the first of many chapters in Taylor's life and career.

At MGM in the 1940s and 1950s Taylor was the model studio actress. A lovely girl was polished into an extraordinary beauty. Foregoing traditional education, she looked to MGM and the movie set and learned the mechanics of acting and living the Hollywood life. The portrait studio was as important in the formation of Taylor's early career as it had been for her predecessors Garbo and Crawford. Even as a child she spent patient hours in front of the portrait camera learning the intricacies of the process. Taylor worked with the best practitioners from the start, and logged many portrait sessions with Eric Carpenter (1909–1976), one of MGM's top photographers in the 1940s.

Taylor left MGM at exactly the moment when the candid snap replaced the studio portrait as the primary vehicle for creating and sustaining a star's image. Early on she proved to be as photogenic in front of the paparazzis' motor-driven 35mm cameras as she had been before the portrait galleries' large stationary lenses. Taylor the movie star was replaced by Taylor the celebrity. And as a celebrity she knew no equal.

From the 1960s onward, Taylor took responsibility for controlling her own publicity. Like stars of the '20s and earlier, she arranged portrait sessions and selected photographers for whom she wanted to sit. One of her favorite set photographers was Gianni Bozzacchi, who worked with her on many films in the late 1960s and early '70s. She also posed for fashionable portraitists such as Cecil Beaton (1904–1980) and Milton Greene (1922–1985). Not Jackie, not Diana, not Madonna—no one else was as richly portrayed, relentlessly pursued, or capaciously documented as Elizabeth Taylor.

*Elizabeth Taylor,* cat. no. 87

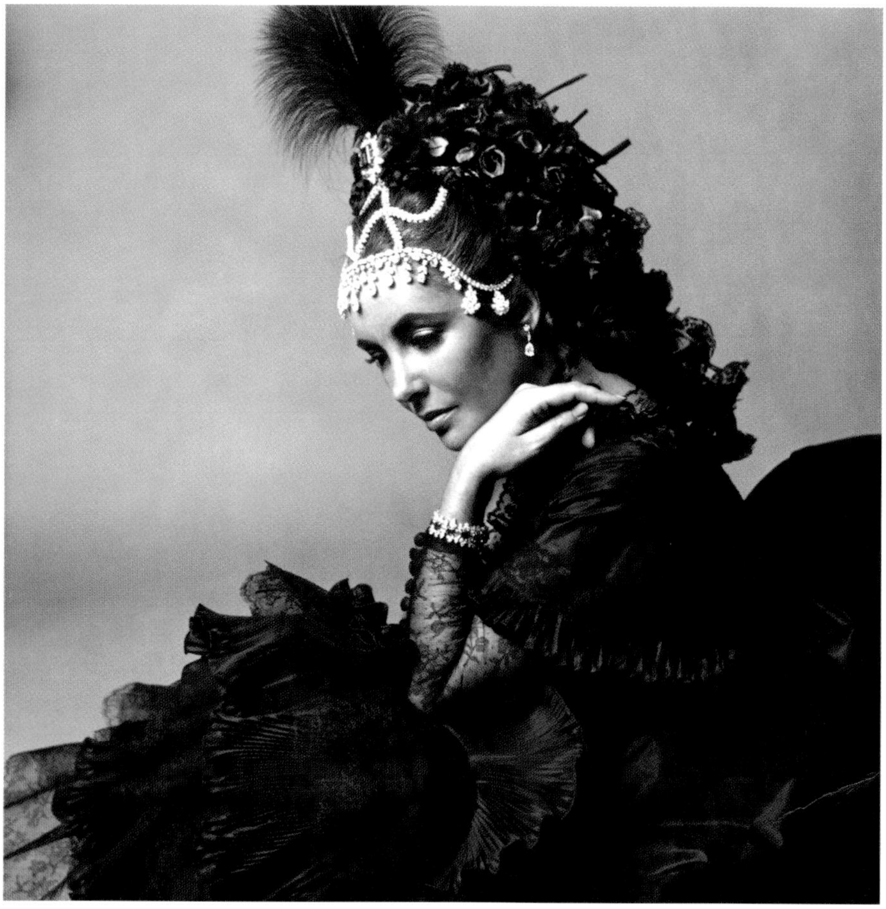



84 Eric Carpenter, *Elizabeth Taylor,* 1944, for *National Velvet,* gelatin silver print, 13 x 10 inches

85 Davis Boulton (London), *Elizabeth Taylor,* 1949, for *Conspirator,* gelatin silver print, 10 x 8 inches

86 Virgil Apger, *Elizabeth Taylor,* 1951, gelatin silver print, 10 x 8 inches

87 [Photographer unknown], *Elizabeth Taylor,* 1968, for *Boom!,* gelatin silver print, 14 x 11 inches

88 Cecil Beaton, *Elizabeth Taylor dressed for the Rothschilds' Proust Ball,* 1971, gelatin silver print, 9½ x 9⅜ inches

89 Milton Greene, *Elizabeth Taylor,* 1974, for *The Blue Bird,* C-print, 18¾ x 13 inches

90 Gianni Bozzacchi, *Elizabeth Taylor,* 1974, for *Ash Wednesday,* gelatin silver print, 10 x 8 inches

*Elizabeth Taylor* (above), cat. no. 89
*Elizabeth Taylor* (opposite), cat. no. 85
*Elizabeth Taylor* (page 70), cat no. 86

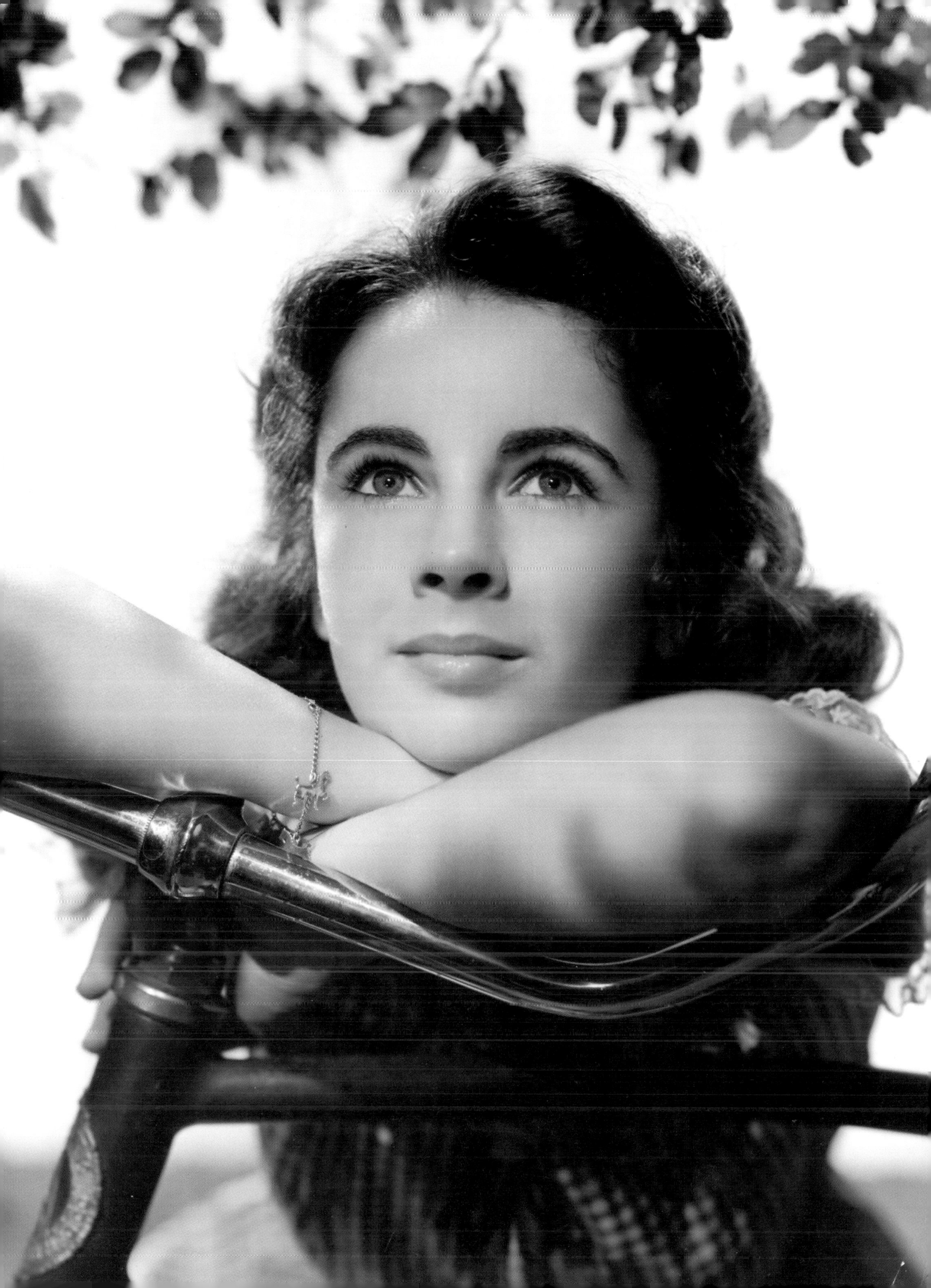

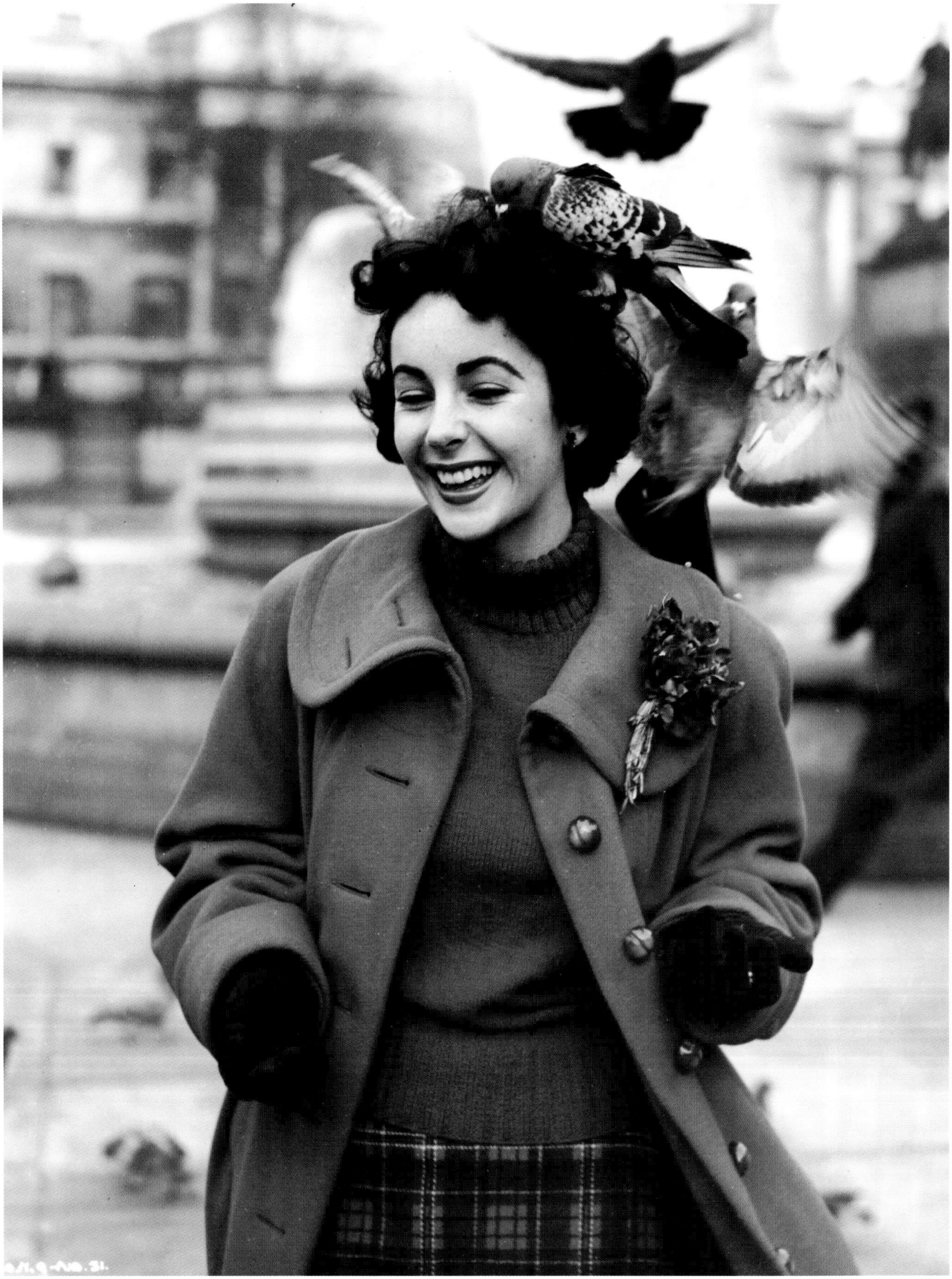

Published in an edition of six hundred copies for members of The Grolier Club.

*Silver Screen/Silver Prints* was set in Adobe Garamond Premier Pro
and Koch Antigua. It was printed and bound by Goulet Printery,
Barkhamsted, Connecticut, on Sappi McCoy Silk White.

Edited by George Ong and Robert Dance
Designed by Margery Cantor